★ ★ ★ ★ ★

FROM BROKE TO SUCCESS

JASON GRESCHUK • JONATHAN LIPSON • DEREK LOEPP
NAUREEN PUNJANI • KEVIN KOZAKEWICH • NELSON CAMP

Printed in Canada.

Written by: Jason Greschuk, Jonathan Lipson, Derek Loepp, Naureen Punjani, Kevin Kozakewich, Nelson Camp

Book design by: Dean Pickup

ISBN: 978-1-9990823-0-7

Table of Contents

★★★★★

Introduction

Where are you going? How will you know when you've arrived?

Have you ever felt like you knew exactly where you wanted to be in life and business, but you couldn't seem to get there? You're not alone.

There's a time when each of us has had to make a decision to take a risk and put all our chips on the table to achieve success, whether that be in business, health, finances or relationships. Some of life's greatest achievements come from taking calculated risks and stepping out of the comfort zone.

Most of us want to start at the beginning ... but sometimes the best place to start is at the end. We want to help you design your personal road map to achieve your dreams.

So what is your dream?

Where do you want to see more success in your life? Health? Wealth? Happiness? Success in each of these areas can be more easily achieved when we discover how the entrepreneurial life can create freedom, and produce surprising advantages.

Entrepreneurs are unique visionaries that not only create profit for themselves, but also often pave the way for the success of others through job creation and the development of innovative ideas.

What are your goals as an entrepreneur?

Maybe it's not to be rich, or build a multimillion-dollar entity, but no doubt, if you're reading this right now, you're interested in success. Success is simply being a winner at whatever you do in life. Success is defined differently for each one of us, but everyone agrees it's a positive thing. Furthermore, it can be achieved in many aspects of life and is not simply a measure of financial prosperity. Someone can also be successful in relationships, have an abundance of time, enjoy good health, or happiness. That's why you need to define success for yourself, just as each of us continues to work daily to create success and enjoy what we have achieved.

Entrepreneurship begins long before a business physically exists. It begins as a small seed, idea or dream; with consistent care and hard work, it can grow.

Like you, each one of us has walked a different road and has unique skills in life and business. But that's the beauty of sharing best practices. Take what speaks to you directly and apply it to your own life.

Entrepreneurial dreams often grow out of a desire for change, to invent something new, to generate income and wealth, or solve a problem. But what happens when you find yourself struggling to make that initial dream a reality?

The best antidote to feeling Broke[n], hopeless, or overwhelmed, is to be creative, work smart, and plan for Success.

We're here to tell you not to give up; build on your ambition so that it becomes one of your greatest attributes.

The best antidote to feeling *Broke[n]*, hopeless, or overwhelmed, is to be creative, work smart, and plan for *Success*. There's great opportunity for growth and reward on the road ahead!

Modern day culture makes entrepreneurship sound sexy (and it can be!), but it takes a significant amount of perseverance and commitment behind the scenes to make a vision become a reality. As you navigate the rough and constantly changing terrain of your business, you will celebrate victories, but you will also experience challenges.

If you are flexible, creative, and willing to face the inevitable obstacles that arise, you will you be equipped to overcome those difficult times.

> “*Connecting with other entrepreneurs can be a catalyst in your life, as it allows you to cross-pollinate, to help one another, and to create relationships based on accountability.*”

Who are we? We are a group of entrepreneurs just like you. We continue to learn, grow, build, and become better at what we do every day. For us, the mission for self-improvement is a passion bordering on obsession!

It takes a specific set of skills and character to successfully build and run a business. The authors you meet in the pages of this book have all spent time thinking, planning, creating, building, and navigating the business battlefield.

When we first met, each one of us was on a different path in our entrepreneurial journey. Like you, our dreams started with an idea and we experienced setbacks and victories along the way. We connected initially through business networking and, after exchanging ideas and learning from one another, we decided to collaborate to share what we've learned. We have done this to create something to help you along your journey in entrepreneurship.

We discovered that as different as we are, we all share common traits. We are as much alike as we are different. Connecting with other entrepreneurs can be a catalyst in your life, as it allows you to cross-pollinate, to help one another, and to create relationships based on accountability.

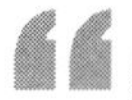

> *the difference between success and failure is in the people you surround yourself with*

The process of becoming a successful business owner is a daily endeavor. Although it can feel frustrating at times, it will also be exciting. If you are passionate about your dreams and committed to the process and the outcome, nothing can stop you!

We wrote this book with you in mind.

When you embark on something new, *the difference between success and failure is in the people you surround yourself with.*

Advice is never hard to come by, but *great* advice is! Who will you be listening to? Friends, family, and co-workers probably won't be able to give you the direction you need. As fellow entrepreneurs along this journey, let us walk beside you, to help you overcome the fear and hesitation of pushing forward to achieve your dreams. Each one of us has been there.

The difference between reaching the summit in your business, and falling into the chasm of lost effort and resources, is often in knowing where to find the support you need.

Why should you read this book?

1. *Everyone benefits from learning from the experiences of others*. As you read about our successes and failures, apply this wisdom to your own life. Try to emulate the lifestyle of the entrepreneur that most inspires you, while also applying lessons we've learned along the way.

2. *Setbacks happen* [it's only a matter of when]. Set realistic expectations and prepare for setbacks in advance. The stories within this book will be a resource for you to draw from if you find yourself feeling stuck or lost in the wilderness of business ownership.

3. *Commit to lifelong learning*. Wisdom is gained when preparation intersects with experience. The experience element does not have to be your own; learning from others can be just as valuable. You will experience the joy and pain that come with success and failures. Look at the entire process as a function of lifelong learning.

If you're new to entrepreneurship, keep in mind that someday your knowledge will benefit others. As you expand your dream, others will benefit as you share your own experiences. If you're a seasoned entrepreneur with several tools and life experiences under your belt, this book will feel like home to you. Use it as a reminder to keep on going, glean some new tactical strategies to implement, and improve your systems. Thank you for reading this book. We know it will enrich your business and accelerate your journey to greater success.

No matter where you are right now, *From Broke to Success* is about the journey and process of learning, self-improvement, and building a successful business. Read about our struggles, best practices and successes, as we share with you some of the greatest lessons we have learned about entrepreneurship.

JASON GRESCHUK

ENTREPRENEUR; REAL ESTATE INVESTOR

BUILDING PEOPLE AND BUILDING COMPANIES

Jason Greschuk began his business career out of necessity after the loss of his father. His first foray into business was as a franchisee for a student based painting company at 21 years old, where he set records that still stand today. Promoted to the position of district manager with the same company for the next two years, Jason oversaw and provided business consulting to 25+ franchisees across Central Canada and, in doing so, oversaw millions of dollars of business every year. Leaving the franchising world, Jason founded Stratford Price, an investment company that acquires businesses and real estate. The first venture in his portfolio was in a realm he was very familiar with, commercial painting. Thus, Stratford Price Painting was founded in 2014. In the same year, Jason also launched Stratford Price Capital, his real estate company.

Jason understands business owners, and specializes in helping owners make sense of the pressures on them personally and professionally, guiding them toward the best decisions. He is passionate about helping owners develop sound principles that lead their company to create a culture of loyalty and commitment, a business philosophy Jason calls "business romance." Jason and his team also specialize in structuring companies, so they are designed to produce predictable profit. Jason's skill set can be summarized in his ability to grow people and companies.

Jason enjoys a close relationship with his family and friends. Along with his older brother Ryan, and mother Grace, they launched Greschukboys.com in 2019, an organization dedicated to helping men maintain fun and adventure in their lives.

Jason is from Winnipeg, a fun-loving entrepreneur, writer, and sports enthusiast with contagious energy.

★★★★★

The Unbreakables

Let me ask you a question. What is the biggest challenge you'll face as a business owner or leader? Hindsight is 20/20. Wouldn't it be great if we all had clarity and insight in advance, so that we could avoid land mines and obstacles? But that's just not the way life is. There isn't just one obstacle, but more of a series of defining moments. The life of an entrepreneur is complex, exciting, and mundane all at the same time.

If you've been in business long enough, you know that there really is no specific roadblock that one can point to as the common challenge we all face. There are many roadblocks, every day. There are many victories too. At the heart of all of it, are two things: process and people. First, you must be willing to set personal boundaries of your own. If you don't, you will get frustrated and overwhelmed easily. With that in place, remember also that other people will always be integral to your process.

I called this chapter "The Unbreakables" for a reason. What I'm about to tell you are some of the principles of how people work and think. Consider them like the laws of nature. These are things I've learned along my entrepreneurial journey and although I do not know it all - by any means - I have still learned a lot. There are certain laws of handling people that become apparent throughout the process.

Everything you'll do in business involves someone else.

People are the answer, people are the problem, and people are the solution. My hope is this chapter will help you gain some clarity about the frustrations you may experience when it comes to dealing with people.

Laws are meant to be obeyed, for the benefit of individuals and society. That's their intent. Without laws and values it would feel like the Wild West.

When working with people, it's fundamental to first recognize certain laws. Laws are meant to be obeyed, for the benefit of individuals and socicty. That's their intent. Without laws and values it would feel like the Wild West.

Take for example, the law of gravity. If a person walks on top of a 10-story building and adamantly declares "I DON'T BELIEVE IN GRAVITY" and jumps off, even if they scream "GRAVITY ISN'T REAL" all the way down, they'll soon learn that they were wrong.

What does gravity have to do with success?

Gravity is real. It exists. No matter how much a person denies it. So, remember, there are laws you can't break. You can only break yourself against them.

Here's the quick list of my favorite business philosophies, and why I call them "The Unbreakables":

1. People never like to be criticized or be told, "You are wrong."

Get used to this and don't tell people how wrong they actually are. Or at least, if you do, keep reading to find out how people respond to that approach. It's not good.

People are much too different, with varying ideas and beliefs - to agree on everything. You will disagree with many people. So, if you disagree with a person, how do you get your point across AND strengthen the relationship?

Here's a fun game: The next time you are in a circle with a bunch of other people talking, listen to a conversation where there is a debate going on. Watch what happens when one person tells another person, "you're wrong," When people are told that, they are usually caught off guard.

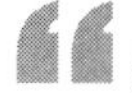

Remember, EVERY statement ever made comes filled with its own set of assumptions.

Their first natural reaction is to justify HOW they are right. They might twist what they originally said to create a scenario where "what they actually meant was..." If the person repeats that they are wrong, they feel more uncomfortable and, depending on their personality type, they will become silent (secretly resentful) or confrontational (openly resentful). Listen and watch for it.

They are usually hurt, especially if they are told they are wrong in front of other people. Being told they are wrong usually arouses resentment and bitterness in the person after the fact. People don't like feeling "stupid" in front of others. Depending on their personality type, they will get confrontational right away or they will internalize it, hold a grudge, and talk about it with people they trust later in private.

Either way, it weakens your relationship with them.

Instead of blatant disagreement, the best thing to do is to ask questions with the intention of truly understanding the other person, and the thought process they went through to get to their conclusion.

Leadership requires patience and awareness.

Behind every person and every statement they make, including every word they choose, is a story. A person whose life has followed a certain track has allowed that track to form the foundation of their belief systems. They've experienced life differently than you and they have developed a different set of beliefs along the way.

Ask them why they think the way they do, what makes them believe what they do, or how they came to that conclusion. Remember, EVERY statement ever made comes filled with its own set of assumptions.

When you help guide someone to reveal all of those assumptions, showing them that perhaps not everyone else makes the same assumptions they do, true understanding will occur. Only from this desire to understand can you actually understand someone on a different level. People like to feel understood.

Most people (mature people, anyway) don't expect everyone to agree with them on everything. They have enough life experience to know that people will disagree with them.

Disagreement is fine, but EVERYONE likes to feel understood. Understand?

When I'm communicating with someone and we disagree, I always try to remember that it might be me who needs to challenge my belief systems.

I find that if you want to make your point known, start by saying, "I could be wrong, but..."

And then make your point.

By buffering your statement, you give the other person the option of telling you that you are wrong.

This gets your point across so that both parties feel respected. People are smart. If you make your point this way, they know where you stand. Additionally, since 93% of communication is non-verbal, they can see by HOW you delivered your message that YOU are concerned about how they feel.

The funny thing is that even if you lead by giving the other person the option to tell you that you are wrong, (because of your tactful delivery), they perceive your humility and rarely tell you that you are wrong!

They will appreciate your humble approach and you'll have a powerfully open discussion.

At the end of the discussion, you may both still not agree, but if you approach the other person in this way, the other person will remember HOW YOU MADE THEM FEEL. You made them feel respected.

This is important. Most of the time it's more important than the actual content of the conversation. Again, mature people know that disagreement is inevitable, and mature people don't try to change other people.

This whole principle can be summed up in this simple proverb: "A man convinced against his will, is of the same opinion still."

People don't like to be told they are wrong. Lead with sincere questions and interest.

2. People hate to be sold, but they love to buy.

This is one of the healthiest attitudes you can have when you are trying to sell anything, whether it is an idea, product, or service. I'll start by explaining it in the context of selling a product or service.

However, before that, try imagining a world without money. It's hard to.

Money is power. Money is an enabler of dreams.

I think it's safe to say that most people are generally trying to improve their situation, and many feel a sense of discontent with their current situation. It's only when we're dissatisfied that we have reason to do anything at all. That's a basic rule of motivation. If you see a person moving around, driving, shopping, working, exercising, or doing anything really, there is motivation behind those actions to improve their state in some small way.

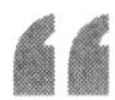

So, if you're in sales, remember this, people hate to be sold but they love to buy. People WANT TO spend money because they see it as the easiest way to solve their problems.

Even watching someone scratch an itch is evidence of this.

Life requires daily problem solving. People always have new problems. People have something stopping their progress. Or they see things they want that their friends have. Or they have a fear of loss. Or a fear of missing out. Whatever the reason, I think it's safe to say that people often try to eliminate the pain their problems cause.

So, if you're in sales, remember this, people hate to be sold but they love to buy. People WANT TO spend money because they see it as the easiest way to solve their problems.

The people who say, "I'm just browsing," are just trying to get comfortable in a new situation. Give them some space. But understand that they HAVE A PROBLEM. And they WANT TO FIX IT. People avoid salespeople because they are: 1) Afraid of being "fooled" or taken advantage of, or 2) not confident approaching new people and starting a conversation, or 3) not sure if the salesperson will actually care about them and their needs enough to make them feel comfortable opening up.

Regardless, people like knowing they arrived at the decision on their own. It appeals to a FUNDAMENTAL need within people to KNOW that they are making THEIR OWN decisions. If a salesperson asks a ton of questions, educates, shows options, and makes the buyer handle their own objections, but ultimately reaffirms the prospect's independence and decision-making ability, the prospect is a lot more emotionally invested in the purchase and WAY more likely to buy because it was THEIR idea. See what's going on?

"I'm saying NEVER think sales is a dirty word. Feel good about selling. Look at a person and see that they have a problem. Recognize that they don't have the information or connections to fix their problem."

People want to spend money. They want to say yes to a solution to their problems. As I stated earlier, they have a deep fear of being taken advantage of or making the "wrong" decision (and having people ridicule them for it).

So what am I saying?

I'm saying NEVER think sales is a dirty word. Feel good about selling. Look at a person and see that they have a problem. Recognize that they don't have the information or connections to fix their problem.

That's why they NEED you. Go help them, whether they want to spend money OR they've accepted that they NEED to spend money to fix a problem. Create a mindset that what you have to offer is so valuable, that it's a gift. Why wouldn't it be valuable if you're so dedicated to it? Remember, you have something to offer your buyer.

Spending money is never really the issue. They've accepted that they're going to have to pay something. And they pay in accordance with the value (real or perceived) that they think they are getting. It's your choice about how you want to package that value for them.

Think of the last time you bought something. Assuming you had a great sales experience, you left feeling RELIEVED, ecstatic, excited, proud, or something of that nature!

I find it hilarious that prospects and salespeople play these games with each other. I think they all watch too many movies. Let's get real. As a salesperson, I want to make money. As a prospect, you want a problem solved and you accept that you have to spend money. So, let's do business.

When working with people, you quickly realize they are always trying to do what they think is best given their situation.

This may sound obvious, but many times I find myself judging another person's actions, instead of attempting to understand.

Realize this: every second, every minute, everyone, everywhere are trying to do the best they can, given their situation.

It is easy to judge. And we all do it.

We look at another person and assume we know why they are doing something. We ask (ourselves – never them) why they aren't doing it differently.

I'm not saying this to judge people who judge. I'm saying this because I think we all need a reminder to stop being so afraid to talk to people and develop the courage to get to know a person without trying to "fix" them.

If you see someone doing something and there is a better way, here's a thought:

If they knew the "better way", they would be doing it!

Before you go tell them the better way, make sure you take

a look at yourself and remember that there are areas of your life that you WANT to do better in. It's probable you have your own insecurities too. So how would you like someone to approach you with a "better way"? Try to use empathy and give your feedback in the way you would like it delivered to you.

I'm sure you would want someone to get to know you first, with no expectations. You would want someone to affirm your effort and desire. You would want someone to admire that. You would want someone to ask questions while sincerely trying to understand your thought process. AND THEN AFTER ALL THIS, you would want someone, probably in private, to suggest, show, or tell a personal story about their life, to help you see a different way, while still affirming in you that it's your decision to choose what you want to do.

HOW we communicate is so important. People are emotional and great ideas or potential are sometimes snuffed out because a person doesn't have the strength to withstand criticism. Don't be one of those people who disobeys this rule. You will only repel people instead of attracting them to you.

Keep these ideas in mind after observing someone and before talking to them. Then go talk to them if you want. Build a relationship. When the time is right, here are some questions you could ask:

1. "Hey, I just saw you doing 'x' and I was curious to understand why?"
2. "Wow, we think differently. Where did you learn to do that? Tell me the story."

The topic of human nature is huge. This information is just a start!

★★★★★

Breath & Blood: The Biggest Business Victory of My Life

There are certain victories in business you always remember. I want to share the biggest business victory of my life.

In the summer of 2006 and 2007, I was a painter for a friend who was running a painting franchise. It was fun work. I loved the people I worked with and the work was satisfying. I had the ability to take something drab and make it look beautiful. I also got to work outside with my friends.

I have countless stories from those times that still make me laugh. And I still keep in touch with my co-workers from that time. Alas, summer 2007 ended and my friend decided not to run the franchise anymore. I didn't feel like working for anyone else, so I moved on as well.

A year and a half later, in July of 2008, I received a phone call from someone in the franchise company. It caught me off guard. A man was on the other end of the phone. We'll call him Jeff. Jeff introduced himself and told me that the company was looking for franchisees to run a painting business for the summer of 2009, and he asked if I had any interest. As the company considered me a great painter, they figured my habits and work ethic might translate into business.

I was caught off guard. I was scared. I told him that I wasn't interested and that I would ask my friends to see if anyone else was. Jeff said he would check up on me in two weeks to see if any of my friends were interested and to see if I had changed my mind.

The truth was this was the opportunity I was asking for. Yet I still came up with all sorts of reasons why it was a bad idea and a good idea at the same time. I remember how nervous I felt thinking about it.

The question haunted me for the full two weeks. I couldn't think about much else. I mean, I wanted the opportunity, and now that it was here, I was freaking out.

Jeff called me back two weeks later. Decision time.

Let me be clear. I was still freaking out. I was still scared.

I told Jeff I hadn't found anyone, but that I wanted to learn more about what being a franchisee would be like.

He met with me numerous times and educated me. I asked every question I could think of. When there was nothing left to talk about, he looked at me and said "Jay, we want to offer this to you. What do you say?"

Something inside me wanted the adventure, I figured I would follow the franchise systems, and do my best, whether it succeeded or not. I paused and then calmly said, "Let's do it."

That was August 2008. There wasn't much to prepare from August to December of that year.

However, towards the end of the year I had already started to have problems. I was in the middle of a business degree at the University of Manitoba. By late December, I had run out of money and had to drop out.

Plus, coming up was the summer of 2009, when I needed to start my painting franchise.

The expectation was that from January to May I would work on my business part-time, doing things like door knocking, dropping flyers, making phone calls to set-up, receiving training, creating, following up on estimates, doing interviews to hire people, and learning the franchise systems.

So rather than spending money going to university, I decided to get a job to earn money to invest in my franchise. Plus, I had no money, so the decision was actually easy. After all, it takes money to send out marketing materials, drive around, and be on the phone.

So, I got a job working as a demolition man for a couple months for a restoration company in Winnipeg. Houses would have some disaster occur (fire, flood, mold, etc.) that would require an insurance company hire us to restore the house. We would also have to preserve as much of the home's content as possible, to be brought back, cleaned, tagged, valued, and reported back to the insurance company so they could put a dollar figure behind the losses the family sustained.

Every day my jobsites were in houses that were burned horribly, had sewer back-ups, or were infested with mold or had some other kind of problem.

Tyvek suits were common. Respirators were a must. It was dirty work.

At one point, I was in a kitchen in a horribly burned house, shoveling through the two feet of burned crud (insulation, wood, and drywall) that had fallen from the ceiling, trying to figure out whether the melted plastic bits I was holding were a $10 Kodak camera or a $200 digital camera.

Everything was scary. The work was new. The people were new. The expectations were new. And this was just a job! Think of how much scarier it would be to run my own business!

At the same time I was working, I was also doing what needed to be done in the pre-season to prepare for running my painting franchise in the summer. Here, everything was even more terrifying!

In January of 2009, the franchising experience started by sending me to formal business training in Calgary. This is where I got to meet the upper management, have someone explain the systems to me, network with other franchise owners from all over Western Canada, and get to know Jeff, the district manager who recruited me.

Being at the training was easy. Having been in university for a few years, the "classroom" environment of the business training was something I was familiar with. Here, everything was textbook. When the training weekend was over, I said goodbye to my new friends and flew home, ready to get started.

No more training. No more safe environments. No more role-plays. It was time for me to take action and find the paying customers. Many people before me had proven the business worked. But I knew that the business would work only if I worked.

Now, out in the real world it was totally, absolutely, 100% different. The franchise company wasn't kidding. They told me they would train me and support me, but it would be up to ME to go out there and do what I was trained to do. It was MY business after all. It all depended on me.

Picture this: it was a bitter, cold day in February of 2009. I had a day off from work. I had already gone through my set-up meeting with my district manager. In the meeting, we had set goals for the year, and he had outlined expectations again about how to be successful, and we had set a pre-season schedule for me about what to do and when.

Yet, I was staring at my computer screen at home, looking at my weekly schedule. I knew what I had to do. It was right there in front of me. I couldn't hide as much as I wanted to.

Sitting on my couch, I reflected on the fact that I had gone through training. I had studied. I had a copy of all the systems of how and what to do. I had a district manager to support me when I had questions. I had a plan. The franchise company had done their part. It was time for me to do mine.

I looked out the window again. Snow was swirling in front of the window. I flipped the TV to the weather channel to confirm how bitterly cold it was, with a wind chill cold enough to freeze unprotected skin in minutes.

That night was the first scheduled door-to-door cold calling session of my business career. I had never cold called in my entire life. And when I say cold calling, I mean knocking on doors, introducing myself to homeowners, and asking if they were interested in getting a painting estimate, to book a spot for the following summer.

I was scheduled to do this for two hours. It was a weird feeling. No more training. No more safe environments. No more role-plays. It was time for me to take action and find the paying customers. Many people before me had proven the business worked. But I knew that the business would work only if I worked.

It was a defining moment for me. Was I all talk? Or would I do what I said I would do? I began to put on my jacket and boots.

What I want to make clear is that I was very afraid. I knew I was about to freeze my butt off AND be rejected ... a lot. But also, I was hopeful I would get leads. I felt fear, but I chose courage and walked out the door.

What do really courageous people have that we don't? I mean, think about it. So many books tell you the secret to success is simply to go out and take action, and they're right. Fear will always be present when you when you are doing new things or find yourself in uncharted territory. A fear-based decision will always be an option in life. If you're doing new things, expect fear to be present. But what is different about the person who feels the fear, and does what they need to do anyway?

They have motivations that outweigh the fear. Some people's motivation is a desire for fame and admiration. Some are motivated to improve their life through money. Some people are motivated by defeating others through competition.

I'm not going to lie to you about my motivation, because I need to be truthful about my story. I had a mix of all of those, but my main motivation was gratitude and a belief that I was loved.

My dad died when I was 18. I didn't know what to do. I needed guidance about what was important in life. I had no idea what to do and in what order. I had a great family and many good friends, but I was missing a mentor.

While my family had gone to church throughout my youth, it was something I never took seriously up until this point. The Bible includes passages about God being a father, and I decided to give Him that place in my life as a Fatherly influence.

I began to read His thoughts about me. I got to know Him. I had doubts, like in any new relationship, but I gave God a fair shot and kept trying to understand him, like you would with any person you want a relationship with. I began to look at how He makes decisions. As I learned, I began to see what He values and how He values others. And I fell in love with what He values. Through quiet time alone, He helped me make sense of my world and I knew I was important to Him. Jesus represented everything I wanted to feel: courage, love, strength, humility, forgiveness, wisdom, acceptance, non-judgment, perseverance, and faith in the future.

I had the right things appear in my life in the form of mentors, guidance, good books, courses, contacts, job opportunities, and the like. Don't get me wrong, I made the decisions and these opportunities were always out there, but the courage to act came from the belief that I was loved. These are key phrases from the

Bible that helped me build my courage: (Jer 29:11), that He had good plans for me (Phil 4:19), and that His natural design for me was to be filled with power, love, and a stable mind (2 Tim 1:7). It's easy to act when you know you're loved. I found truths, believed them, acted on them, and uncovered character traits I always had. I didn't have to work hard to convince myself I had changed. I just chose to believe the truth I was reading from someone I trusted. This helped motivate me for two years in jobs with very little recognition. These were my private victories.

Remember this. If you ever see me and wonder why I am the way I am, it's because I have many people to thank. First and foremost, I thank my mother for teaching me how to have faith and showing me unconditional love. And my brother for always caring about me.

I've had many wonderful mentors in business and life. Entrepreneurs need someone to go to when they get overwhelmed, and for me it's been God and godly people. Behind closed doors, my life is the result of a constant, authentic conversation with God where I'm earnestly learning about who He is, and who He says I am. And let me tell you, it gets better every year the more I learn.

That's where I get my validation. Not from social media likes, stacks of money, or my face plastered on a magazine.

In no way am I trying to alienate you. You don't need to believe what I do. I simply can't lie to you about what drives me and what my story has been. Whatever your motivation, it has to be greater than the fear that will push at you.

So here I was, standing in the freezing cold outside, ready to travel door-to-door. I was ready to work. Even though I was scared, I stood outside on my front steps feeling ready to provide for myself, my future team, and my family.

It was cold. Every door I went to unveiled a different scenario. Some people were angry I was letting cold air into their house.

Some thought I was too early in the season and they weren't thinking about painting. Some were not interested but encouraged me to push forward. Some were annoyed I bothered them during dinner. However, most importantly, a few wanted a painting estimate! And a few was all I needed.

From that one session in 2009, I was motivated to push forward to the end of the summer. I had knocked on hundreds, if not thousands of doors, taught others how to cold call, hired staff, managed clients, ran payroll, marketing campaigns, developed good habits, and earned quite a bit of money.

> *Don't complain about why you don't have more clients. It will do you no good and perhaps just add to the harm. It means you're too far removed from the trenches. Get back in there. Go get rejected. It's good for you. Every no gets you closer to yes.*

I ended up setting a record in Manitoba for the highest producing franchise by a rookie franchisee in the 30-year history of the company. This record still stands today.

Here's the lesson: If you have breath in your lungs and blood in your veins, you can go and make money.

Sales isn't as hard as you think. In fact, it's pretty cool that people live in homes. It means you know where they are and you can go sell them something.

You get the idea? You're surrounded by money. You're surrounded by people you can help with your goods or services.

If you have a pulse, you can go make money. And I HIGHLY recommend you do cold calling for extended periods of time and do it consistently for months or years on end. You learn so much about people and yourself.

And more importantly, when you have more established companies, and you begin to doubt yourself and your ability to sell, you can always remember the victory you felt when you started with NOTHING, walked out the door, and made money anyway.

Don't complain about why you don't have more clients. It will do you no good and perhaps just add to the harm. It means you're too far removed from the trenches. Get back in there. Go get rejected. It's good for you. Every no gets you closer to yes.

This realization alone, this internal piece of gold, makes all the fear, courage, rejection, and success worth it.

I gained the ability to feel fear and continue to push forward anyway.

Now I had hours, weeks, and months of experience, feeling fear and choosing to do what my goals and motivation pushed me to do.

The crazy thing is, once you realize this, you can't lie to yourself anymore.

When you have a victory in an area once, (in this case, cold calling), you know that you can do it. Build on that confidence and success. Also, if you need to do it again, you really don't have an excuse. You have done it once and can do it again. This is the strength of the entrepreneur. Vision and action. Entrepreneurs are action-oriented thinkers.

I'm not saying cold calling is the best way to market your business. I know there are smarter ways to market yourself. That's not what this is about. It's what cold calling did for me personally that made the difference.

It taught me that business is a numbers game.

It taught me that the business is ALWAYS out there.

It taught me that fear is an illusion. It's only a suggestion.

It taught me that I can make money when I have nothing.

It taught me that I was willing to do whatever it took.

Every successful entrepreneur can tell you how much they cherish the realization that they don't need much to make money. They know how to start anything! They just need the breath in their lungs and the blood in their veins. If that sounds like you - chances are you're a serial entrepreneur.

Essential Habits of Entrepreneurs

There are things you must learn as an entrepreneur that prepare you for success. And with so much information in the world and so many things to get distracted by, sometimes it's hard to know what habits are worth spending your time developing. Once you become aware of all of the habits that make you excellent, you also begin to see similar habits in other entrepreneurs. I have done a lot of learning and growing along the way. I have also tried to learn the strategies and habits of others. From that, I want to share with you essential habits you will need no matter what you do for work or for your career.

I'm so passionate about this. I can't even count how many times I've shared the unbelievably powerful, yet simple ideas in this lesson, and yet people gloss over them like they aren't important. Don't let that be you.

> *One thing is certain, the journey through life will teach you about yourself. With enough trial and error, you will begin to see what you're good at, what you love to do, what problems you like to solve, and you will be able to see the area/industry/type of work you were MEANT to dominate.*

Read the following words carefully. In this lesson, I'm going to drop two "truth bombs" on you that will change your life.

Here's the reality: You will likely do many things in your lifetime. Your interests will change. Your job will change. You might start multiple businesses even. You may fail big once in a while!

One thing is certain, the journey through life will teach you about yourself. With enough trial and error, you will begin to see what you're good at, what you love to do, what problems you like to solve, and you will be able to see the area/industry/type of work you were MEANT to dominate. However, I believe there are certain skills that EVERY person must turn into unconscious habits if they want to carry their dreams into reality.

Are you ready? Here's the first truth bomb that will serve you no matter what you do in life.

Truth Bomb #1: I've decided to become MILITANT about following the idea below:

Do What You Say

When I was 21 years old, I ran a painting franchise. It was my first real, organized business experience. "Do What You Say" was part of the company mantra the parent company taught. I love how foundational and simple their mantra is. It isn't complex. It isn't terribly profound, but my experience has been that so few people actually LIVE by this principle.

Franchising was such a great decision for me. Up until then, I was reading many books but I didn't have a vehicle to test my "head knowledge" in the real world. What I was finding was that I was so uncertain and it took a REAL challenge like franchising for me to prove that I was more than just book smart. This is how anyone makes REAL change:

It. Starts. With. A. DECISION.

I decided that, no matter what the results were in the franchise, my highest priority was to I do what I said I would do.

The cool thing about running a franchise is the company literally tells you how to succeed. They give you a book on how to run the business. "Do this," they tell you as they hand you the operations manual.

Since I had a proven system, I didn't have to put much mental energy toward figuring out the business. I was 21 at the time and I had A LOT to learn about business. But, the technical side of how to run a painting company was right there in front of me, in black and white.

So, I put my mental energy toward learning how to be a better goal setter, planner, and seeing every decision, every moment, as an opportunity to make promises to myself (setting goals) and make sure I fulfilled those promises. It was a great training ground.

Here's an excerpt from my book *Business Romance* which summarizes my thoughts on this:

"If we focus on doing what we say with respect to ANY goal or commitment (and I mean any...no matter how big or small), think of how powerful our lives would become. Think about it. Imagine if you were able to 100% believe the words and promises that came out of your mouth, every single time? How powerful would you become? You would LITERALLY be unstoppable and any dream you verbalized would be acted on confidently. Why? Because, through training, you are always willing to pay the price and do what you say when you commit to something. On the contrary, if we never believe the words we say, we will struggle to see our value, we will not take our goals seriously (might as well not set goals at all then) as no goals will ever be accomplished, and we will float through life just wishing things were better.

Doing what you say is an expression of faith. We humans are wired for faith. We are wired to see things in our mind before they exist in front of us. EVERYTHING that exists today was a thought or picture in someone's mind who dared to dream it AND take consistent action. Think about that for a second. They had faith. Anything we dream up, we can see. Since we can see it, we can write it down. Anything we write down can be broken down into actionable steps for us to complete. Repeatedly taking those steps WILL get us to that dream. If this is all true, there is nothing in our way.

Here is a fun game you can play to improve your integrity using numbers:

1. Get out a printout of a weekly calendar. If you use a calendar on your phone that's fine too.
2. At the bottom of each day, write the words Reflect and Reward.
3. Every night before bed, think back on that day. For EVERY statement you made where you said you would do something and followed through, give yourself 1 point. For every statement you made where you did not follow through, give yourself 0 points.
4. Total the sum of your successes, and divide them by the total opportunities you had. Multiply it by 100 to get a percentage of how often you followed through.
5. Reflect at the end of every day.
6. Always try to get a higher percentage today. If you do, reward yourself.

No matter how big or scary a goal is, every goal in the world can be broken down into smaller, more manageable steps. For example, a yearly goal might be broken down into monthly, weekly, daily, or even hourly smaller goals. This method keeps the goal from feeling overwhelming and helps you focus on what needs to be done right now.

Remember, each one of us can only live one day at a time. We only need to FOCUS on doing what we say ONE DAY AT A TIME (i.e. today). If the goal is huge, life isn't fighting you. The only thing goals do is TELL US WHAT IS REQUIRED FROM US EVERY DAY to experience the life we want to achieve with that goal finished. You don't like what the goal says? Then don't set it so high! Simple. But if you want something, you have to be willing to do what is required of you EVERY DAY.

No one in life forces us to believe this. We must see for ourselves how powerful this works in our own lives, before we decide to be militant about never letting this principle escape us.

This is so, so powerful. If we accept that we are already people of integrity, at every opportunity we have, we will follow through with what we say. That way, we can say whatever we want and our identity will compel us to fulfill our promises.

This is one of the core values of my company, Stratford Price. I want to build a culture of leaders who do what they say.

So, what have we learned?

Every decision matters. Every – Single - One. Each decision is going to reinforce a habit, good or bad. Remember our goal is unconscious integrity. You said you'd pick a friend up at five? You'd better be there at five! You said you would finish that report tonight? Guess who is staying up late! You!

I just dropped a bunch of amazing information on you and you might be loving it or you might be intimidated by it. Now it's time to take the plunge, to put what you've read into action.

Many times I've had people agree with me, they don't actually make the changes. I want you to make the changes. I want you to make progress. So, if what I just said about integrity is theory, here are the practical steps to make integrity automatic for you:

1. Accept a general structure for your day. Accept right now that, in order for you to reach your goals in every area, you need to set aside time EVERY DAY to do tasks that get you closer to your goals in every area of life. From a practical standpoint, how else will you get there if you don't take bite-sized chunks EVERY day? For example, I have a yearly goal spreadsheet that I update before the New Year starts. I have goals for everything. I have spiritual, business, reading, fun, giving, health, and investing goals. Create a schedule for your day.

2. Print the words "Do What You Say" and put them everywhere you frequent throughout your day. In the bathroom, at the kitchen table, in your car, or perhaps on your desk. Leave no place out. Put these words everywhere. Do what you say, and keep your word.

3. Now that you are equipped with these tools, think your goals through. Write them down in every area. Fill in the spreadsheet.

4. Then, pull out your day planner, which shows all the hours in a day, and figure out the best time to devote towards getting closer to your goal in EVERY category. Fill in your daily schedule and weekly schedule.

Now that you have your daily/weekly schedule on paper and your yearly goals in a spreadsheet, how do you remain consistent on a DAY-TO-DAY basis?

1. List Goals, Set Priorities. Label your priorities in order of importance. An A priority is the most important. These are the items that MUST be done today. B priorities are next. C priorities are those that are okay to do tomorrow if you run out of time today. Be flexible because your priorities may have to change during the day.

2. Start your day with your daily To-Do List.

3. Complete your A priorities first. Then tackle the B's. Then the C's. Adjust and re-prioritize as needed.

4. Handle each task only once.

5. Learn to say no.

6. When it's time, do it immediately.

7. Always ask yourself, "What's the best use of my time right now?"

8. Remember, your workday starts the night before.

Every night, before you go to bed, you should reflect on your activities. Now look at what you said you would do. Do they line up? Remember to differentiate between results and effort.

Most people, even the most successful entrepreneurs, wake up in the morning with a list and tackle the list. Often there are email interruptions, calls, and staff interruptions. What I'm suggesting is vastly different. I am suggesting beginning your day not just with a list, but with specific goals in mind. When you know exactly what you want to accomplish that day, you will do it. The reason you will do it is because you are a success already. You are a successful human and a successful entrepreneur. It's my belief that most people fail because they haven't learned how to tackle their day with intentionality. I'm giving you the tools right now to do just that.

RESULTS depend on your SKILL in doing the things you say, while EFFORT is central around actually SHOWING UP, starting on time and finishing on time. Results will get better as your skills get better. Just get in the habit of being able to answer yes to the question: are you doing what you said you would do?

Look at your goals before bed and make a plan for the next day. Write out your plan for the next day with 1) what you are doing 2) at what time. Essentially, you are creating blocks of time to do certain tasks to get closer to all your goals.

Do not go to bed until you have done this.

Unclear on your priorities? Check your goal spreadsheet again. It should tell you.

Now, I get it, you may be thinking "Wow, that's a TON of work."

Yes! You're right!

Remember how I promised you two truth bombs? Here's the second one:

Truth Bomb #2: The sooner you accept that life is work, the better off you'll be.

I'm not talking about your job or business. I'm talking about life. The natural process of anything on this earth is death. It takes work to save it. Not convinced? Consider this:

What happens if you never talk to your significant other? Answer: the relationship dies.

What happens when starve yourself of healthy food? Answer: your body dies.

What happens when you don't LEAD change in your business, innovate, and commit to constant improvement? Answer: your business becomes obsolete, competitors find ways to serve customers better than you, and your business dies.

Not doing anything at all is easy. Anyone can do it.

It takes work to build strong relationships.

It takes work to get educated about healthy food and how to get it.

It takes work to exercise and keep your body strong.

It takes work and effort to study people and see how your business can serve them better.

If you want ANYTHING worth having in life, it's going to take work. As the pastor at my church says, "Any dead fish can float downstream, but it takes a mighty strong one to swim up."

The lesson? Learn to love work.

Remember, set goals that are meaningful to YOU! The goals you've set are YOUR goals! YOU want them! Not me. Not anyone else.

If you HATE work, one of two things are happening:

Your vision is not strong enough.

A stronger vision makes self-control easy. Don't focus on self-control. Focus on making your vision something you love to dream about. Remember, you can have a vision and still work for someone. It means that you are seeing each task as an opportunity to learn new skills, cement those skills, and cement good habits to PREPARE you for that upcoming promotion when it comes. Promotion could be within the business you work for, or a promotion could be you deciding to start your own business. Bottom line, life is opportunity. And opportunity favors the prepared. For your sanity, also remember to stop often and give yourself credit for the wonderful habits and choices YOU made so far, and forgive yourself for those choices that were not so good. Being able to encourage and celebrate yourself is essential to progress to the next level.

Or, if you hate work, the second thing happening is:

You are living out someone else's vision.

Make sure the goals you set are YOUR OWN. This actually takes more work than you may think. You need to reflect on your past, your skill set, what you were doing when you felt passionately alive, etc. Remember, you don't have to jump into your specific "dream job" TODAY. You can simply start by acknowledging what situation you excel in, or the type of work you enjoy and place yourself in that environment. Wherever you're at, keep your dream white hot by spending time with it. There are likely many things to learn and character traits to develop before you're ABLE to handle that dream job or dream opportunity when it comes around. So be prepared. Have faith. Look for the opportunity.

Another excerpt from my book *Business Romance* may encourage you:

"So, if we choose the path of using work to live on purpose, what does all the above have in common? It will take MORE EFFORT than letting life happen to you and just "getting what you get." It takes WORK to reflect on our pasts. It takes WORK to forgive others and ourselves so we can move on, accept new beliefs, and make new choices. It takes WORK and courage to set new and challenging goals, to try again. It takes WORK to make time to DAILY review your goals. It takes WORK to write a vision for your future about WHO YOU ARE, so you can start being that person NOW. It takes WORK to fill your mind with thoughts and beliefs that will help you and us be successful.

These beliefs are like a muscle. The more you work it, the stronger it gets. Always be on alert. Remember, in front of you are always two paths, every hour of the day: The one YOU choose or the one of where you allow life (people, the past, parents, friends, naysayers, the media, etc.) to tell you what to think and believe. Take control of your mind. As for us at Stratford Price, we live on PURPOSE about everything in our lives, we don't live by DEFAULT in the way our parents, friends, upbringing, or culture programmed us initially."

Life is work. You either work to enjoy a life you dreamed up and DESIGNED, or you work to repair and fix a life you didn't design and is full of things you don't like(unfulfilling relationships, lackluster business, poor health, etc.). I use this system to stay very organized so I can run two multi-million-dollar companies, AND still have a life. AND still have my health. I'm here for you! You can do it too.

★★★★★

Three Skills to Invest in That Will Always Guarantee You Income

Over the past decade I've experienced several things in business, in quite a few different roles. In my early twenties, I was a great performer. I ran my own franchise, while following a proven business model. In my mid-twenties, I became a great coach and business consultant to franchisees all across central Canada. Since then, I've started two businesses on my own from scratch and I've grown them into multi-million-dollar companies.

I've cold called. I've knocked on doors. I've had people quit. I've been rejected thousands of times. I've hired people. I've let people go. I've had people steal from me. I've made bad investments and had bad days. I've made great investments and had great days. I've known what it's like to struggle to make payroll.

I've sold or have helped others sell millions of dollars in services. I've personally bought and sold millions of dollars of real estate. I've also raised millions of dollars for real estate joint ventures in my local market, and I've learned how to lead myself and other people so they absolutely love to work with me. I want to hit pause here for a moment to tell you why I've told you all this. I'm just an individual like you, learning as I go. Like you, I started with a vision and I have put in a lot of hard work. I'm not a superhero and neither are you. And that's OK. I'm a regular guy doing amazing things because I'm learning each day and I'm taking action on my learning, which is what this book is all about. You may have experienced every one of the things I'm talking about or none of them at all.

I've dealt with many difficult people over the years (clients and employees) and it takes a lot for me to get stressed out about it. In fact, because I have time-tested beliefs about business, money, and people, stress is not a constant experience for me like other entrepreneurs I know. Now don't get me wrong, life is not always perfect.

It hasn't all been sunshine and rainbows. Far from it. Business has cost me over a million dollars in the form of much needed investments into my businesses, as well as business coaches, and MISTAKES.

Why am I telling you all this?

It's not so you can praise me. Or so you can pity me.

I'm telling you all this because I've had enough life experiences that I can confidently tell you in this chapter what THREE SKILLS you need to develop that will NEVER become obsolete. These three skills are worth investing in. You'll need them no matter what. So, listen up!

The world is changing fast, and this will ALWAYS be the case. Get used to it. Industries, jobs, the economy, these will always change as we move forward in the future, and it's going to change at an increasingly faster pace. If you have any arguments with this, become a student of history and see for yourself. Humanity has insatiable creativity and a desire to innovate. We must all decide how we want to change and LEAD CHANGE. Someone's going to do it. Is it going to be you?

Naturally, our innovative society causes some industries to die while new industries are born. This means new jobs requiring new skills.

This is not a bad thing. I'd go so far as to say it doesn't matter what you or I think about this truth. What's more productive is that we just accept this truth.

“Whether it is a product you're trying to sell to a client, or a group of employees you're trying to sell an idea to, your ability to make other people like you enables you to "print money" for yourself your whole life.”

With that being said, I believe there are certain skills that can be DEVELOPED that will NEVER become obsolete. Here they are:

1. Ability to build relationships
2. Sales skills
3. Ability to interpret failure

Let's start with the first one: Ability to build relationships.

If you can feel comfortable walking up to a total stranger every day of the week, introducing yourself, making them feel great about you, making them feel great about themselves, being memorable, and gaining that person as a friend who will pick up the phone the next time you call them, you can succeed in any industry.

Whether it is a product you're trying to sell to a client, or a group of employees you're trying to sell an idea to, your ability to make other people like you enables you to "print money" for yourself your whole life.

The reality is people have problems. People use money to solve their problems. People WANT TO spend money. Money is their solution mechanism for whatever their heart desires. Combine this truth with the fact that people only buy from people they like and trust, and you understand it is essential to learn how to build relationships with people, and in doing so, you enjoy life, and the people in it, AND you guarantee your income.

If this is something you want, consider the timeless principles outlined in the book *How to Win Friends and Influence People* by Dale Carnegie, one of the best books on relationships ever written. For time's sake, I'll only go over the first three. I encourage you to check out the entire book.

Principle #1: Don't criticize, condemn or complain.

Remember this. No one wakes up in the morning and deliberately tries to do something wrong, do poorly, or bring pain into their life. Why on earth would someone do that on purpose? They aren't doing it on purpose. What's the only other answer?

The only other answer is that everyone thinks they are right. Remember, everyone, everywhere, every second of the day, is always trying to do the best they can and do what THEY think is right. Why would people purposely do something wrong? There may be some information they are missing. Remember, in learning how to build relationships, don't make your sole focus their mistakes. To build a relationship, see the mistake and be curious. Ask them about the thought process that led them to what they are doing. Ask them questions to help them find a better way. Protect their confidence and reputation and you will have won them as a friend. The other option is choosing to be critical of someone. If you do this, they WILL get defensive. They will likely be hurt and it may show up as passive-aggressive behavior or aggressive behavior. You will now have gained an enemy.

In their mind, who are you to say they are wrong? They think they're right and their life path has led them to the beliefs that are shaping their life. It's my belief that people want to do better. They want to be respected. So give them that. Be curious, not critical. It doesn't mean you have to hire them, do business with them, hang out with them, etc. But you should respect them, no matter who they are. Perhaps the words of Abraham Lincoln are a good reminder: "I would be the exact same person they would be under similar circumstances and upbringing."

Here's what criticism does to people: It only makes them defensive, arouses resentment, hurts their pride, and hurts their self-importance. People WILL respond like this. So how much good is your criticism actually accomplishing? If your goal is to work with them through a problem, your criticism isn't helping you make progress.

So, next time you're talking with someone and they say something you don't agree with, don't tell them they are wrong. Even if you are right, you don't actually win because "a man convinced against his will is of the same opinion, still."

Instead, ask questions. Explore their train of thought. Acknowledge HOW their point makes sense. Remember, your goal is never to win, it is to make them feel good about you. At this point, you have made them feel understood. It is from this point on that the other person likes you, because you have made them feel good, and now they WANT TO hear what you have to say. If there is improvement to be made, people WANT TO make those improvements. They want to do it in an environment of acceptance and respect, where someone believes in them and makes them look good.

Principle #2 - Give honest and sincere appreciation.

Appreciation matters. A lot. Here's a thought to help with this: How many people actually live out their crazy boyhood or little girl dreams? Some dream of being an astronaut. Some dream about being a pro hockey player. Some, professional singers and dancers.

What percentage of people never end up working in their dream career? 99.9%. That's not an actual statistic of course. Maybe it's higher than that. Maybe you and I are in the top 5% or maybe 1%, but one thing I know for sure is that many people with childhood dreams never achieve them.

So, if people aren't getting fulfillment from the career itself, what is giving them fulfillment? The vast majority get it from being in an industry they find interesting, solving the problems they like to solve, surrounded by people who admire them openly and make them feel important.

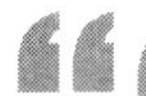

The more you learn to love yourself, the more ability you have to love others and give honest and sincere appreciation freely.

The desire to feel important is the deepest human need.

So how does one make it natural to genuinely and generously praise people?

Answer: The more you learn to love yourself, the more ability you have to love others and give honest and sincere appreciation freely. The more you love yourself and your ability, the less threatening people are to you. If you are secure in yourself, it's no skin off your back to recognize and appreciate people, and in doing so, you build relationships and create trust.

On the Business Romance Academy website, I host a weekend course to show the personal journey I went through to create a book about myself that summarizes and combines all my life experiences, skills, personality, temptations, and my vision about life and business. It energizes me. It centers me.

In short, I know myself. And I love myself. And this allows me to STAY FASCINATED with myself and others.

This is what allows me to love others and give honest and sincere appreciation. This is what has enabled me to have a HUGE network of people who enjoy our connection. If you have trouble meeting people, consider downloading a cue card I made called "Keep Calm and Network On". To give you a little teaser of what's on the cue card, here's a quick list of three things to help you love others:

1. Every person alive today is 100% unique. No one has existed exactly like them before ever in history, and no one will ever exist exactly like them again.

2. Everyone, everywhere, every hour of the day is always trying to do the best they can with what they know. Give them credit for their effort.

3. People crave unconditional acceptance and they will give their loyalty to people who accept them.

Principle #3: Arouse in them an eager desire (insatiable want).

I love this one. Acceptance of this truth makes it so much easier to create win-win situations that build relationships.

Staple this to your forehead: The only reason anyone has EVER done anything since the START OF TIME is because THEY WANTED to do it. So, find out why it would be in their best interest to do something and only speak in terms of that.

I challenge you to go out on a day this week and be an observer. Go into a crowded street corner and watch people. SOMETHING compelled them to get up that morning and show up and start shopping. Why? We can't fully know just by looking. We'd have to ask them. The point is that in business and life, relationships are built by:

1. understanding people's problems.

2. painting amazing mental pictures of solutions (...your solutions) to those problems.

3. and encouraging their decision-making ability.

Here's the truth: Never talk to people about what you want. Yes, know what you want, but don't talk about it. Always talk in terms of what the other person wants. Show them only how they get what they want by working with you on your idea, project, transaction, etc. because that's all they care about.

What does this require? Asking questions and listening. Make sure you ask questions, emotionally engage with the person's story and reasoning. CARE about them, and listen to the words they choose, how they say them, and their body language.

Doing this makes the other person feel listened to. They feel heard. They feel important. Now that you understand their problem, show them a solution...YOUR solution.

Not only will people love how you listened to them and valued them, they will now see you as the one who helps them solve their problems. You will be seen as valuable to them and they will want to continue the relationship.

I'll make this next one easy for you. I've never been big on tactics. A lot of people focus on some kind of system for mastering control of other people. That sounds exhausting. I suggest you just find truths about people and believe them. Life is much easier this way.

Here's the truth about each individual person:

Each person you meet today is 100% unique. There has NEVER been anyone just like them in the past and there will NEVER ever be anyone just like them in the future. This is the truth.

Picture yourself at a networking event. Everyone there is a gift to humanity. Humanity is graced with their unique selves. And you have the privilege of meeting each individual.

Have you ever considered what a privilege it is to actually KNOW another human being? You are complex. People are complex. Relationships are sometimes the most frustrating things on earth, but also, if nurtured properly, can be one of the most fulfilling things on earth.

This is amazing!! Knowing this, how can you NOT treat people with absolute curiosity? What they think, what they feel, and what they value becomes something you have the privilege of knowing.

Also, did you know one of the most commonly used words in the English language is the word I? What does that tell you?

That means that every person, most of the time, is thinking about themselves. If you take a genuine interest in other people, they will remember you as the person who gave them a chance to talk about themselves, the person who made them feel important, and they will absolutely want to talk to you again.

You might be saying, "That's easier said than done".

Yes and no.

If you find this difficult, it may be that you're too self-centered, insecure, and out to prove yourself, which is a form of insecurity. If so, welcome to a frustrating life. The cure for that is to realize how much help you've actually had along the way, know you have a lot of people to thank as the reason you are where you are now, and realize that your gift cluster is unique and no one can do exactly what you can do as well as you. So, don't be threatened by others. Now, marinate in that, love yourself, and go take a genuine interest in other people.

Let's move on to sales skills.

Picture where we are now. We have mastered the principles of building great relationships. We genuinely enjoy each other and feel a mutual understanding of each other. It's in this environment of trust that it is absolutely NOT wrong to give the person an opportunity to buy your solution.

Sales will always be needed. No one has full knowledge of every topic available on the earth, and no one has the time or ever will have the time to educate themselves on everything. In that, people rely on salespeople and they always will.

If you think sales is a gross word, you will struggle in business and life. Every employee in a business is either in sales, or supports the sales team in some way. You need to see sales for what it really is: caring about people and solving problems. As Rabbi Daniel Lapin says in his book *Thou Shall Prosper*, commandment #1 is, "Believe in the dignity and morality of business."

What is the first line item on any income statement? Answer: Revenue. What is revenue? Revenue is sales. If there are no sales, no business can afford to give people a salary. In short, selling is essential to life. People need salespeople to listen to their problems, and then educate them about solutions.

Some of you may be saying, "Automation is going to make salespeople obsolete." Sure, some positions may not require salespeople anymore, but then copywriters of sales pages and the content/sales funnel creators still have the skills to write words that sell people solutions. Decentralization still requires people to sell other people on ideas.

The bottom line is, sales skills will never be obsolete. There is not enough time in this book to teach you everything you need to know about sales. They have great courses on that. I've said this before, but it's so crucial that it needs to be repeated. People hate to be sold, but love to buy. Give them every reason to buy from you.

As well, people are generally insecure about their money and their ability to make decisions. They hate feeling like they've been duped or taken advantage of. They want to brag at dinner parties about how smart they are because they bought a certain thing, and they want to recommend you. Be a great product/service provider and help people make decisions (i.e., be a good listener, be good at unearthing objections, handling them, closing, and re-closing.) People need help making decisions.

Another thing to remember is that people like simplicity. Make your solution simple and make sure it requires no work on the customer's part. Give them the royal treatment.

The last skill to master is the SKILL of interpreting failure. Yes, it's a skill. How will you view your failures?

Every day of your life, you have gained the most experience you can possibly could have gained given who you are. This present day, the day you are reading this, you are the BEST you have ever been at ANY point in life. TODAY, you have never had more experience, you have never had more knowledge, and you have never had more of a network than you do RIGHT NOW. And you probably failed a bunch of times to get there.

However, do you feel the best that you can be? Or are you cynical?

On businessromanceacademy.com, I have authored an e-book you can download called *Identity – The Key to Effortless Change.* It is part of a larger course you can take. Having a strong sense of identity is the key to all success and progress. In this e-book, I talk you through a process that helps you determine why you are the way you are, what you can do to find mistaken beliefs that are giving you bad results, and finally, it helps you understand how to actually BUILD the right beliefs. Every entrepreneur needs a support group – these are people who you can share your thoughts and feelings with, who will listen without judgement. They don't have to be family. If you're having trouble finding them, they are out there. Keep looking.

Be honest about your feelings with those support people – and by honest I mean fully honest. You need to get it all out. Lack of honesty is fear. And fear is not the foundation you want to build your life on.

Take ownership of those feelings. They belong to you and it's okay to feel them. They are a sign you need to do something. Feelings are seldom wrong. You should get to the bottom of why you feel the way you do.

Take ownership of your choices. Accept that, regardless of how you felt, it was still you who made the choice, and it was still you who put yourself in line to receive the consequence (good or bad). Even if you say others "made you do it", they didn't. Stop giving other people control over you. Set boundaries in your life regarding what your responsibility is and what it is not.

Bottom line, when you fail, you have to take ownership, forgive yourself, do your best to reconcile with others if needed, write down what you learned, talk about it with your support group, and begin encouraging yourself to go in a new direction with new information.

Encouraging yourself is also a skill. It means re-affirming new decisions you've chosen, re-affirm that they are one- step in a direction to what you want, and that you have the ability to make that choice every day.

The last thing I'll say about encouragement, you need to encourage yourself like the way you eat food; you must do it daily.

Take my word for it. Most people don't realize they are giving up on their dreams until they have. Stay sharp. Speak the change you want to see.

Talk about your dreams a lot. They give purpose to mistakes. The reason this skill will make you money is that, if honed, no matter how many times you fail, you will try again. This is worth it because without YOU making choices and taking action, YOU will never get anything.

These three skills are worth putting effort into and will never become obsolete. Investing in them will never be a waste of time. They will ALWAYS be good investments. Make time to grow in these areas!

★★★★★

Turning Your Business from a Job into a Cash Flowing Asset

Most entrepreneurs struggle to turn their companies into assets. Most grow their business and trap themselves in it at the same time. They grow and operate their business in a way that the business NEEDS them. This forces the owner to work all the time and they can never step away and enjoy the lifestyle they envisioned their hard work would result in. Let me tell you, it is possible. As the owner, you have to see yourself as a business builder AND as an employee of your company.

In this lesson, I'll tell you how I built two companies AND removed myself from them. Let me tell you from experience, you HAVE to be intentional about how you spend your time EVERY SINGLE DAY if my advice is going to work for you.

Before you take my advice, here's my resume on building companies:

In 2014, I started a painting company with one broken arm. Five years later, it became a multi-million dollar operation employing 20 people. The business makes great profit even after paying myself a great salary. If I decided not to grow or do anything different the rest of my life, I could maintain this six figure salary, my business could maintain a multiple six figure profit , all while

I only have to work part-time hours each week. Pretty good for a labor-intensive service company!

And that's only one of the multi-million-dollar companies I have ...

I also started a real estate company in 2014 and grew it to a multi-million dollar company alongside my painting company over the last five years.

Don't get the impression that any of this was easy. It was incredibly difficult. It took a lot of time and energy. I made a TON of mistakes. I have lost money many times. I had personal relationship problems that I had to overcome. I had many disappointments to rise above. Looking back, I will say that it takes a lot of vision, personal management, people management, strategy and energy to build a company, and turn it into an asset. But you can make a salary and you can make profit. AND you can do it without sacrificing your health and relationships. Despite the hardships, building these companies was so worth it. And you CAN do it too, no matter what industry you're in.

That's exactly why I want to suggest some ideas to you, so you can do it too, and create freedom for yourself.

Let me paint a picture of my day for you, so you can see what it's like to be an owner whose business is a cash flowing asset.

Let's take a normal Monday for me. I split Monday working hours into two types of work: Business Maintenance and Business Development.

Think of Business Maintenance as me earning the salary I pay myself by doing my job description in the business. This is the time in the day I see myself as an employee of my business.

BUSINESS MAINTENANCE

7:00 a.m. – Generally, I start the day by coming in early to remind myself of my personal and people management habits (7 Time Management Rules, 4 Habits, Principles of People Management). I also spend some time with my written vision for both the business and my life so I'm so pumped to get started on the day.

8:00 a.m. - Then I look at all our bank accounts, accounts receivable, accounts payable, and where we are in relation to the annual budgets we set at the beginning of the year. I am able to pull up all this information because we have calibrated our software program to run reports for us like this.

In addition to this, all of this information syncs directly to our financial statements so the majority of our financial statements are populated automatically. This way we know exactly how much money we are making all the time.

> *Let me be clear on this. Whether it is in marriage, business, family, teams, whatever it is, the ONLY person you can truly be responsible for is yourself. Your feelings, your choices, your emotions, your beliefs, your words, your actions, etc. You can't control other people and you shouldn't try.*

I make note of positives, like where we are hitting or beating budgets and who is responsible for that, so I can congratulate and reward them.

I also make note of negatives, like where we are over budget, accounts receivable dragging out, missing bill payments, and anything else to help me predict cash flows better and let me know who needs coaching through their tasks.

I take these notes with me to the next part of my day.

8:30 a.m. – I prep for meetings with my staff. I'm in the position right now where there are people in place who I have recruited that perform all the tasks needed for the business to run.

10:00 a.m. – Have meetings with the people who report to me. The point of these meetings is to guide the staff in my business. Again, I have all the job descriptions I need, and I have filled those roles with great people who know what is expected of them and have similar values to me. It's my job to take the raw person and help build them into better leaders, better salespeople, better managers, better office professionals, etc., through clear expectations. It doesn't matter what they do, it's my job to help them clearly learn their strengths, their role, expectations that come with that role, and the rewards that come with meeting or exceeding those expectations.

Other things I do to prepare for the meeting is review the nature of their personality and review past meeting notes. After all this prep is done, I make an agenda for my meetings with my staff that follows a similar structure to this:

1. I make sure they know I'm human. I tell them what I'm excited about in my life, and I ask them what they are excited about in their lives. I use this as an opportunity to share my vision with them regarding the things I am working on in the business, and what it could mean for them.

2. I bring up topics they are excelling at and tell them very specifically HOW what they're doing is making things better for themselves and the company. We go over goal spreadsheets, which show what targets they are trying to achieve and review what they are actually achieving.

3. I bring up topics they need coaching on and how what they are doing is hurting themselves and the company.

4. I ask them what ideas they've come up with from last week to fix the problems they have.

5. We make plans with deadlines to fix the problems they have.

6. We leave an open spot at the end to talk about anything at all.

In effect, this is how I set boundaries and teach my staff to set boundaries. This is the healthiest thing you can do in a business.

I want to pound this point home. In order to build a business that gives you freedom, you have to be an expert at: 1) defining what you, and others, are responsible for and what you, and others, are not responsible for, and 2) communicating it in a way that shows appreciation for people (you can't do it without them) and tells them how their role is important.

Let me be clear on this. Whether it is in marriage, business, family, teams, whatever it is, the ONLY person you can truly be responsible for is yourself. Your feelings, your choices, your emotions, your beliefs, your words, your actions, etc. You can't control other people and you shouldn't try.

Another thing to remember in your relationships with another person, you may be responsible TO them, but you are never responsible FOR them.

For example, when you say your vows and get married, you agree to share your life with that person and support them in many ways. Both of you are now one. In a marriage, it's a real gift to have that person you can trust deeply. You have one person you can be yourself with, talk with, cry with, dream with, strategize with, and share the ups and downs of life with. Along the way, you may need that person to be your shoulder to cry on, your booster, and your confidante.

When you need them to be those things for you, it is their duty be there for you, and vice versa. That's them being responsible TO you. But ultimately, after they are done comforting you, encouraging you, and listening to you, YOU have to be responsible FOR yourself, get new information and take actions to make your feelings, consequences, and situation improve. That's called being responsible for yourself.

It's very important to know the difference between "responsible for" and "responsible to". When you look through these lenses, you clearly see when people are attempting (consciously or subconsciously) to violate your boundaries.

From here, you can choose to give because you WANT to give and you can hold others accountable, which is what they need. Know that when you don't hold people accountable, you make their problem your problem, and you will likely secretly feel resentful. And the worst part is that it's your fault, not theirs, because you did not set boundaries.

Bringing it back to business, it's this realization that makes me feel 100% comfortable holding employees accountable for their jobs. The moment they signed the employment contract and CHOSE the job, and the duties and expectations that came with it, is the exact same time I CHOSE to love them by building a great company that gives them clear expectations and training. While also completing regular performance evaluations so they know how they are doing, and rewarding them for the results they produce. Both of us chose each other.

Now you may be thinking, "Wow, that sounds pretty mechanical Jason. What if one of your employees needs help?"

Just because I see a boundary violation, doesn't mean I change my management style and freak out at them. I'm still me. But the recognition of the boundary violation shows me that person needs help and lacks confidence in achieving something. So, they try to pass off the responsibility to a co-worker, or YOU. They lack confidence in some area and it's my job to privately speak words of encouragement, offer training, SHOW them how to do the task, and tell them I believe in them.

It's also my job to HELP THEM talk through the solutions they are thinking of applying to the problems they are facing.

It's my job to set benchmarks and targets, using our budgeting system, to help them learn what goals to shoot for.

It's my job to create a compensation system that rewards them for improving the company, and increasing revenue for the company.

★★★★★

Relationships are Everything in Leadership

It's my job to be certain of key aspects about business and people so I am an attractive leader to my team, and so I communicate with respect and admiration for my staff, regardless of the kind of day I've had. Part of the owner's job description is to be a great leader, and that takes time and energy in a day, but it is an essential part of the owner's role.

It's my job to remind them that when they master the role they occupy, they will be promoted.

It's my job to design a training program that shows a map to their success, clearly outlining the hard skills, and soft skills, they need to learn in their position, and what to produce to get a raise. And if they want a new position (i.e. promotion), I've prepared job descriptions for every position in the company, what is required of that position, and what that position must report weekly to me.

These things are what owners do.

The notes from these meetings go in their specific employee file that contains their employment contract, weekly reporting metrics, personality profile, job description, and past meeting notes.

12:00 p.m. – Lunch

12:30 p.m. - BUSINESS DEVELOPMENT

Business Development is about me building the business to earn profit on top of my salary. This is accomplished by meeting new clients, hiring new recruits, building better business systems, or planning investments in the business. Business Development is anything to improve the CAPACITY of the business. The morning was my time to work "in" the business to earn my salary. The afternoon is my time to work "on" the business to increase its ability to earn me profit, remove some of my risk, etc. Business development increases the potential of the business.

Working on the business can mean many things. For me, I do one or a few of the following:

1. Build new relationships – new clients, new potential recruits.

2. Build culture – read my book *Business Romance* and other good books, and allow creative ideas to come to my mind to express these values (This is fun for me. And I've learned that I NEED to be having fun).

3. Improve company systems.

I also have in my office a DO LIST and a DO NOT DO list tacked to the wall on my left. This acts as a quick reminder, based on my job description and the job descriptions of my staff, not to do someone else's job.

The afternoon is usually a collection of appointments with clients, interviews, or looking at the project list on my wall. Appointments include things like going to networking events, golf tournaments, lunches with clients, etc. My project list is a list of business systems I want to spend money on improving.

The best part? My team is happy I do this and I'm happy I do this. I've been up front with them about what I'm great at and what I LOVE doing: building relationships and structuring the business.

THEY TELL ME to go and do these things and leave the rest to them, because they have chosen jobs they like, using skills they are good at.

★★★★★

Company Structure

To recap, I can run my entire multi-million dollar business by splitting my time between Business Maintenance and Business Development.

I don't have to work evenings. I don't have to work weekends. I haven't succeeded at the cost of my health or relationships.

This was my vision early on. So how did I set all this up? And in what order? Where did I start?

Let's start with the basics. It doesn't matter what business it is, any business has six main components to it: Marketing, Sales, Production, Administration, Recruiting, and CEO.

CEO – This is you. Your values dictate what you value in business. Every business needs leadership. Do you have personal management rules you operate under? Do you manage your personal

> *"I wrote Business Romance to help my company learn what my personal values and convictions are on these topics. In this way, it has proven to be a great launching pad for me to know my staff and allow my staff know me. This builds intimacy."*

finances well? What are your personal beliefs about employees? Do you see them as independent people? Or do you "own" them? Both of those beliefs have consequences. Which one do you believe?

What about beliefs about customers? Sales? Success? Money? Work?

I wrote *Business Romance* to help my company learn what my personal values and convictions are on these topics. In this way, it has proven to be a great launching pad for me to know my staff and allow my staff know me. This builds intimacy. The best definition of intimacy I've heard is "Into Me See." Let other people see into you with your words and actions. And see into them with their words and actions.

Sales – You need to sell your products or services. What is your pricing compared to industry? What product offerings do you sell? What are the costs of sales? What is your average sale size per product offering? How many leads turn into sales for each offering? What is your booking percentage? To run a company, you need to focus on answering these questions.

Toolkit – Software programs can help you easily pull up this information. Do you know how to pull and create these reports? What are your top selling items/services?

Marketing – Who are your customer groups? How are you different from your competitors? What problem do you solve? Do your customers know that? What is your cost per lead for each offering?

Toolkit – Generate ideas for marketing initiatives and set budgets, have a way to track return on investment (ROI), cost per lead, and profit per lead. Until you can answer this with a lead tracking sheet, you don't know what good marketing is.

Admin – This is huge. Can you pull up the files you need instantly? Do you have proper financial reporting in place? Can you say with confidence how much money you made every month? Do you know what your most profitable revenue streams are? Does the answer you give line up with your bank statements? Do you have separate bank accounts set up to house your profit, tax liabilities, operating expenses, owner pay, and income? Read *Profit First,* by Mike Michalowicz to find out more about this.

Toolkit – Creating charts of accounts in accounting software, annual budgets and monetary policy. Your financial policy shows your path to profit.

Production – This is the fulfillment side of your product or service. Do you have defined processes on the best way to deliver your product or service? Are these communicated to your staff? Have they provided input? Are expectations clear? Are there feedback loops from the customer to you so you know how you're doing?

Toolkit – Software that allows you to track the flow of business and communicate internally and externally.

Recruitment and Training – Do people know what is expected of them? Do they have a position mandate? Have they been shown their job description? Do the duties make sense for the role? Do people know what numbers to report on weekly? Do you have training in place for each position?

Toolkit – Job Descriptions, Position Mandate, Compensation Plans, Interview Process, New Hire Orientation, Human Resources Manual, Performance Review.

There isn't enough space in this chapter to talk more extensively about this. If you want to take action because you realize you can't answer these questions, there is lots of content about this on businessromanceacademy.com, where I talk about how I implemented it in my business. Not only that, but we help you realize when it's the right time to implement the proper systems.

There are also podcasts and blogs that talk about how to build your company to be an asset. Do you want to have your company spit off cash for you and give you freedom? I think you do.

Although I don't have all the answers, I do have some. Everything I've written here, I've been through and I can offer you the advice from one entrepreneur's perspective. As you read through it, you may find you're so inspired that you want to rush out, imprint these ideas and close the book! Let me encourage you to take notes in the notes section below, instead. Stay committed to your learning and growth, and continue reading! We are here for you. You'll be glad you did!

Notes:

Notes:

NAUREEN PUNJANI

SERVICE BASED SPECIALIST

A leader, volunteer and problem solver – Naureen believes in the power of hope, collaboration, and building bridges.

Born to a family of modest means in one of the poorest parts of the world, Naureen worked tirelessly to carry herself and her family out of the jaws of poverty and isolation and broke the barriers of violence and judgement.

Pouring into her life and career her personal experience of triumph of endeavor over adversity, Naureen firmly believes in continuous improvement, pursuit of excellence and empowering people so that organizations are able to reach their highest growth potential.

Her qualifications in cost and management accounting and internal controls, along with over two decades of financial management experience in South East Asia, the Middle East, and North America, has helped her contribute meaningfully to the development of organizations she has worked or volunteered with.

After working in various industries, Naureen and her husband Rafiq now own and operate multiple businesses in Canada, in sectors such as bookkeeping and financial management, commercial cleaning franchising, home health care and real estate. They have won multiple local and international accolades for their excellent and record-breaking management skills.

Naureen and her family volunteer a large portion of their time for their community. Naureen serves on board of directors of various community organizations.

★★★★★

Nothing Lasts Forever: Active Change Management

One of the greatest mysteries of life is how impossible it is to find anything that stays the same. Close your eyes and try.

The galaxy, our planet, the oceans in it, animals, plant life, human race, our families, friends, our work and most importantly, each one of us - are not destined to be here forever.

The innate nature of our universe is that it is in a constant state of change. Grasping every single point in that change process is physically impossible to comprehend or be ready for. Change occurs daily.

Even your own thoughts are in constant transition. How you may feel about a person, place, or thing may drastically change over years, days or even minutes! This is perhaps one of the biggest surprises and mysteries of humankind. The change to your inner world — how you once fell in love and years later fell out of love, or how you once craved a certain food that you no longer enjoy.

The continuous transformation we deal with inherently means that hardly any of our experiences will last very long. The time span of these experiences may vary but if we take a bird's eye view of our lives, we can see that our time on this Earth is simply the combination of many short stories we are part of simultaneously. And short stories end.

Our experience as we know it with people, places, or things, always ends.

The amount or form of change we go through can be pretty dramatic. Some of these occurrences are pleasant and welcomed and some come as a complete surprise and leave us shocked.

We are usually surprised when our expectations of the world around us (including ourselves) are not met, when the responses are different from what we had in mind.

As much as we cannot evade or control every single change that we will have to face, it is quite possible to 'plan' for it.

The solution is to harness the skill of Change Management. A solid, well thought out process around anticipating, recognizing, and responding to change.

You may be thinking 'Well, of course I know that!' It sounds like a no-brainer, doesn't it?

Take a minute and think about it. Have you actively invested time sitting down and thinking about anticipating, recognizing, and responding to change?

Actively is the key word here.

1. Anticipating Change:

Whether we are talking about personal life or business, most change is accompanied by many emotions. Anticipating change helps us manage our emotions beforehand and keeps us focused when change actually happens.

Here is a personal example.

Imagine the time when you first met your partner. All you think about is happiness, love and years of being together. The mere thought of not having that person in your life is unbearable and makes you sad.

You do however, at some point in your relationship, visit your insurance broker or lawyer to talk about your will, health care directive, and life insurance policy.

At that meeting, you discuss your partner's potential passing, getting into an accident, being diagnosed with a life-threatening illness, or being in a coma in such detail that you begin to feel dizzy.

While this is a difficult discussion, and is nothing more than an awful thought, the conversation is still extremely important to have right now.

If you have never thought about that scenario before as a couple in an environment that is in your control, and when things are all right, imagine how distraught you will be when and if this actually happens. Preparation is the key to managing this type of change. Without it, things can be a terrible mix of outcomes.

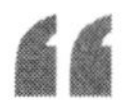

> *Our minds are biologically programmed to sense danger and avoid risk. Without anyone having to ask you, at this very moment you know who or what your business will crumble without.*

You will be without the loving support of your better half, trying to deal with the huge loss, all while having to make important decisions for yourself, your future and your family. Your judgement can be quite impaired. What's the best way to manage change when the change is unexpected? Anticipating it.

Anticipating change doesn't mean that you will necessarily have all the answers or be ready to face change when it comes. It will, however, minimize the emotions that may surface unannounced, when you suddenly face an unforeseen event.

So, how do you 'actively' anticipate change?

We are creatures of habit and get comfortable fairly easily.

Therefore, we must train our brains to 'actively' anticipate change. This doesn't mean we jump to the worst-case scenario and trust nothing, while being worried all the time.

Imagine this hypothetical scenario. There is a key employee who is running your sales department and this person has created a lucrative business for you. Due to this pipeline of sales, your business is booming and you have more work than you can handle. You hire more people, invest in more equipment, and open a second location. Business is great, and at the bedrock of it all, are the sales that this person is feeding into the business.

During these great times, it's important to sit yourself down and actively think of a situation when on a moment's notice this key person may not be there.

Think of the damage it will cause to you and your business. Face this fictional scenario in your mind as vividly as you possibly can. Engage your core management team in these discussions.

Our minds are biologically programmed to sense danger and avoid risk. Without anyone having to ask you, at this very moment you know who or what your business will crumble without. You are already subconsciously planning for the worst, all the time. Actively thinking about these scenarios however makes you take the risk from your subconscious into your consciousness.

Now your brain will be planning for such an event even when you are not aware that you are planning for it.

Actively anticipating this change will allow you to plan for it better. Moreover, when that person actually hands in their resignation, you will not have a sense of doom and gloom as your mind was already being conditioned for such an event.

Most importantly you will not feel like you're dealing with this scenario for the first time, and you will be composed. You will be clear headed.

2. Recognizing Change:

Have you heard the term boiled frog syndrome?

If you put a live frog in boiling hot water, it will jump right out.

However, if you put a frog in water and slowly bring the water to boil, the frog will not register the gradual change of temperature and will eventually die due to extreme heat.

Ask a long-term employee at an organization why they do any task in a particular way. Seven out of ten times the response is, "because that is how we have always done it."

Often times we stop registering the change around us because it is gradual and because we are too focused on "more important things."

You may have done things one way - but that doesn't mean it's the right way.

Apply this example to your business. Often times we stop registering the change around us because it is gradual and because we are too focused on "more important things."

But who decides what the "more important" things are?

As much as bringing in more business, while delivering products and services to your clients is important, so is keeping an eye on changes in the morale of your workforce, shifts in the culture of your organization, technological revolutions and client's varying needs. As a leader and entrepreneur, all of these things make a difference. They all matter.

Equip yourself with the right tools to recognize these gradual changes. You can do so by training your brain to scan for 'trends' in the situations around you, and not mere instances.

Often times we confuse symptoms with the actual problem.

Imagine a key employee who has started to make mistakes here and there. The issue may not be huge right now but if it persists, this change can cost you resources and reputation. Maybe that employee is going through something at home that is temporarily distracting and important, or maybe they aren't. It's important to discover the truth.

Think; can you see a pattern?

Does that employee keep repeating similar mistakes or does this person make new ones each time? The former points to a need for re-training however, the latter may suggest a lack of interest. Each of these two reasons will have a different response to it.

Once you train your mind to see the pattern instead of focusing on individual mistakes, you will know the root cause and offer an appropriate solution.

3. Responding to change:

How successfully you master the first two steps in the change management process will determine how effective your response to the change will be.

This response is a two-step process:

A. Responding to the change *before* it happens:

As part of an anticipating change mindset, vividly think about the event that is speeding toward you.

This active thinking allows you to theoretically live it.

Use that opportunity to plan for things, what will cost to replace a key employee? How can we minimize the damage? Is there anything we can do to extend their stay? Are there alternative staff from your existing team? How can we minimize reasons that may cause this person to leave your business?

This analysis creates a 'proforma process' which will tell you steps to follow when this change hits you. You can document this process as formally as you like. Either way this is something that can become a habit, which you can draw on in the future.

B. Facing the change when it materializes:

Having prepared for it, you have already explored the nightmare a few times, so your emotions won't get the best of you.

However, you will still have some emotions. Try and keep them out of the decision-making process. It doesn't mean bottle them up or ignore them, but simply make a commitment to come back to your feelings later.

For example, when an employee actually quits, say, right in the middle of closing a major sale, reserve the right to be worried, upset or even angry about the timing of the departure, but focus on a solution first.

Refer to the plan you created and alter it based on new information available.

We often hear that the only thing that is certain is change. Still, we are almost never ready, and are surprised when life throws a curveball. Having a group of fellow entrepreneurs available to mastermind with me has been an amazing opportunity to manage the curve balls. How do you expect to manage distractions, stressors, or the curve balls that come flying at you at one hundred miles per hour?

Mike Tyson famously said that everyone has a plan — until you get punched in the face! Isn't that the truth?

As much as we plan, actively anticipating, recognizing, and responding to change, it is never a walk in the park. It is much easier said than done. Complexities of situations and personalities will often derail our best laid-out plans.

The key is to remember that this too shall pass.

★★★★★

Who Does What?

Imagine a modest local bakery on the street corner in a small town. Flowers gently dance in their tiny, wooden window boxes. A crooked handmade welcome sign invites passersby to stop and take notice. Mouth-watering aromas of delicious, oven hot cakes and cookies wafts through the air as the owners – local residents Granny Annie and her husband Jim – tend to the customers, with huge smiles.

Now imagine a bustling corporate headquarters of a multinational billion-dollar business. It has its giant footprint in 165 countries. Busy managers roam the hallways earnestly talking on their phones. There is a general sense of urgency in the air. A bunch of senior executives is occupying one of the nine boardrooms in this eight-story office complex. They are engrossed in a crucial discussion about launching the corporation's operations in a new country.

Seemingly, these two businesses have nothing in common.

Take a closer look and you will find that no matter which business you look at, big or small, the basic areas of focus for the stakeholders are the same. These areas may have differently named 'departments' in different businesses, but the fact remains that each business has, in one shape or another, five basic areas: operations, finance, human resources, marketing, and technology. Together these functions form the core management team of a business, in larger operations, an army of specialized individuals looks after each of these functions. Roles are clearly defined, and chain of command distinctly identified. Departments are segregated, and personnel are often housed, so it is easily visible who is responsible for which of these five basic areas.

In a smaller operation, roles may not be as clearly identified. Often a handful of people – mostly the owners/ partners or their close family members – tend to wear multiple hats. The areas of focus however, remain the same.

Let's journey back to Granny Annie's Bakery.

Jim looks after cash (finance). Granny Annie takes care of the bakery with help of her youngest granddaughter Alexa (operations). Alexa is also the one who paints the welcome signs and decorates the receiving area. She writes specials on the small board by the door and distributes flyers at the weekly farmer's market (marketing). Jim is the one who the young students from the community college nearby talk to when they drop by the bakery from time to time looking to make extra income (human resources). Jim's son, Arthur, makes sure that the till, telephone and internet lines are in working order (technology).

No successful entrepreneur has ever said they have no clue how their business functions. The first step therefore is to develop, focus, and identify what tasks make up each of these five areas in 'your' business.

To facilitate future scalability, it is imperative that you know from the start which elements your business is made up of.

Why do I stress this point so much, you may ask? Let's take a look at a cooking example.

Everyone cooks. You have to cook food to eat. So whether you think of yourself as a cook or not, you are. You may not be a five star chef, but you're a cook. Everyone cooks food. It's like breathing oxygen. In the cooking example below we can see how the elements of what you're working with matter.

When you make soup, the recipe remains the same whether you make it for a family of four or for 300 people for a gala dinner. All you do is expand the quantity of ingredients depending on the number of servings.

But what if you didn't know what ingredients and quantities make up the soup? When you try to expand the soup by 'guessing' its elements, you will run into problems. You will put less salt in it or perhaps more minced garlic. Perhaps you will completely forget to add more onion since you forgot the recipe called for it. You may be able to ultimately slap together a soup for 300 people, but it would be after much wasted time, needless experimenting, and unnecessary headaches. You would taste test, and each time you would make the soup differently.

Many entrepreneurs run their business this same way.

What if, from the inception of your business, in fact from the time the idea started brewing in your mind, you could identify the major areas that would make up the ingredients of your business, and you would then have a better chance of successfully identifying corresponding experiences and get the right resources onboard instead of fumbling around later? This is ideal of course, yet not the normal path for entrepreneurs. Entrepreneurs tend to execute without a plan.

I'm here to help you plan better. To give you insight into additional things you'll need to consider.

Secondly, when you start a business, take time to identify who will be primarily responsible for each of these five areas.

Imagine, in Granny Annie's bakery that Alexa starts writing on the specials board one morning.

However, she is constantly interrupted by Jim and Arthur who are breathing down her neck, telling her to change the specials or use a different style for her writing. This is a common occurrence in every new business.

There are several problems with this approach.

Who is watching the cash register while they are all huddled around the specials board?

Alexa is feeling micromanaged and she is very likely going to make a mistake. Jim and Arthur's intentions are good, but they may be giving bad advice since they were not told what Granny was baking today.

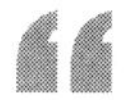

Being open to hearing probing questions from each other, in my experience, is the single most valuable skill that the owners and top management can develop.

If Alexa's job is interfered with enough times, she may stop trying to contribute original ideas. She will lean on others to make her decisions, and ultimately may lose interest in her work due to not discovering enough meaning in her role. She will likely feel as if all independence has been taken from her.

This may sound like a trivial example; however, this is unfortunately an incredibly common mistake new and small businesses make. It can happen in larger corporations as well, but since roles are more clearly defined, chances are individuals have greater autonomy.

Discussion and consultation among operations, finance, human resources, marketing and technology are essential, however, there should be one person in charge of each.

Think long and hard, who on your team is capable (or trainable), to assume leadership for each one of these five roles?

In a smaller organization, or depending on the nature of the business, one person may be able to assume two or more of these roles to begin with, typically a visionary or the leader with a plan. But a leader can't do it all and must eventually rely on the team to execute.

Assumption of these roles typically coincide with the education and experience of the individuals, but also pay attention to what the individual's aspirations are. What areas may they naturally gravitate towards in future? No one wants to wake up one day and find an unmotivated employee in a leadership position.

If individuals are assigned within the roles of their choosing, adjusting to a new role will be one less thing stressing them out, compared to all the other pressures of running a new business. Once settled in, they can always sprout wings and explore new uncharted management roles.

Third, once their roles are assigned, be sure that everyone on the core management team is clear on his or her responsibilities, and span of control. This will allow them to research and keep themselves and others in the core management group up to date. This person will be expected to find answers and initiate discussions pertaining to their area.

It is extremely important for a business that a culture of mutual trust and openness is cultivated. This starts with the core management team.

Being open to hearing probing questions from each other, in my experience, is the single most valuable skill that the owners and top management can develop.

Often, asking for clarification is mistaken for questioning one's qualifications or integrity. This may sound like simply a matter of insight, however being quizzed on one's views and decisions on a day-to-day basis isn't a walk in the park. It requires a conscious and continuous effort. This accountability among top management keeps the organization's blood flowing, since ownership alone doesn't give you free reign.

On the flipside, decision-making processes may sometimes come to a screeching halt if the management team can't agree on the way forward on a decision. This is a critical part of leadership and management. Processes matter.

To prepare for such a situation and to avoid paralysis by analysis, my recommendation is to agree on veto rights from the start.

The assigned person for each role is usually the best choice for this, as they have the most insight or wisdom relating to that specific role. This fact should be respected. They should be allowed to exercise veto in times where the core management team is in a bind, and the only remaining alternative is indecision.

This so-called veto is a privilege but is also a huge responsibility.

Each area manager is expected to be continuously keeping their notes updated and ready to explain to the satisfaction of the core management team the reasons for each of their decisions.

As the organization grows, it becomes increasingly important that the role managers are cross-trained, starting with overlapping matters. This allows flexibility when life happens and critical people leave the company, but also increases soft management skills within the management team. Cross-training also serves as an internal audit, as different people job-sharing creates awareness of risk factors and training gaps.

Lastly, be okay with being wrong.

The core management team should stay vigilant, to ensure that each of the five roles are filled by qualified professionals. Business is more important than individual egos. Despite all the time spent training a role manager, if it appears that an incorrect assignment was made, it is better for everyone to change their role sooner rather than later.

In this regard, the responsible personnel should plan a graceful transition so that the change happens with the least interruption possible.

In summary, you can segregate duties in your small business by following this five-point checklist:

1. Breakdown tasks in your business in five areas/functions - operations, finance, human resources, marketing and technology. Together these form the core management team.

2. Identify one person to lead each of these five roles. In small business, one person may lead multiple areas.

3. Ensure the assigned person understands their responsibility fully and cultivate a culture of openness and accountability.

4. Focus on continuous learning and cross training.

5. Change course as deemed necessary. If you still feel that your business is too small to worry about all of this, remember every decision matters. If you want to be a successful entrepreneur, run your small business like it is a multi-million-dollar corporation. This way it will become one. If you don't want it to, because you're content with where you are in life, run it like a professional company and watch everything change for the better. You'll have more peace, less stress, and more time to engage in the things you truly love. With good systems in place, you will build an attractive asset that can eventually be sold, if that is part of your plan.

★★★★★

How to Successfully Run Your Business .... into the Ground

Warning: Sarcasm ahead

So far, in this book you have read a lot of material on how to be successful. After all, the name of this book is *FROM BROKE TO SUCCESS.*

However, we all love to choose how we become successful. Having a choice gives us a sense of control and independence.

I recently heard a friend say that unlike other parents, she doesn't worry about dressing up her 3-year-old child. She never runs around after the little streaker, trying to put him into his romper. Instead, she places two items of clothing on the bed and lets him choose. The rest is a breeze. Such a simple solution!

An effortless solution is the power of choice. So, let me offer you one.

The purpose of this book is to offer you a multitude of ways to go from broke to success. In this chapter, you get everything you need to know if you want to go the opposite way!

In the next few pages, you will learn how to successfully run your business ... into the ground.

Before we embark upon this journey, remember that like any

other achievement, this will require careful planning, hard work and perseverance.

If you consistently apply the below mentioned ideas and tips, no one can stop you from successfully achieving failure.

From Success to Broke Tip #1:
Completely Ignore Numbers: Do Not Prepare a Business Plan.

In a nutshell, the business plan serves as a crystal ball. As you try to run your business on paper before you start committing a ton of resources.

"Lenders or funders always ask for a business plan to approve start-up or growth loans / grants / investments. At the business planning stage, if your business doesn't make sense financially, it is most likely that it won't stand the test of time."

It documents your projected income over several years and potential expenses that go with it. It allows you to think ahead of time, take into account volatility of income, and tells you how soon you can expect to start making your money back.

Lenders or funders always ask for a business plan to approve start-up or growth loans / grants / investments. At the business planning stage, if your business doesn't make sense financially, it is most likely that it won't stand the test of time.

A well-drafted business plan clearly separates a solid business idea from simply a dream of owning a business. A business plan might not always show positive growth, or the viability of a business, but it will save everyone from having false expectations, so they can start understanding what needs to be done to fix it.

Preparing a well thought-out business plan is a big step towards a successful business. To avoid being successful, you need to side-step this evil trap.

Be sure never to invest any time or resources on it. If you do prepare one, never consult a trusted advisor who may be able to give you invaluable advice towards making your business plan a road map to success.

From Success to Broke Tip #2: Disregard the Concept of Opportunity Cost

Opportunity cost is the loss of potential gain when an alternate path towards potential gain is chosen. It focuses on scanning all alternative paths before you decide the best way.

For example, imagine you provide two different services to your clients. For service 1, you charge $100 an hour. For service 2, you charge $75/h.

If you have only five hours available in a day, and two clients are both interested in hiring you for those five hours. The first one requests service 1 and second one requests service 2 – both due on the same day.

If you choose to deliver five hours of the lower paying service 2, your lost opportunity cost is $25/h x 5 hours = $125.

Another example: Imagine your hourly rate for your clients is $125. You are great at what you do but you have too much work.

This work doesn't just include the billable work you do for your clients, as you also manage your own social media, marketing, and bookkeeping. Both these functions take 15 hours of your time each month, but you can outsource them at $50 an hour. The total cost of outsourcing is therefore $750, but you will save 15 hours a month that you can contract out for $125 an hour to your clients, thus you are making an additional $1875 a month. The net gain is $1125. The opportunity cost of NOT out-sourcing and continuing with the status quo is $1125.

This concept is not only financial. Remember to measure how much not choosing alternative paths will cost you, even if there is no cash involved. For example, the opportunity cost of playing video games versus learning a new skill.

If you want to be truly unsuccessful, you will need to completely remove the concept of opportunity cost from your decisions. This concept helps you make smart decisions, which you definitely won't want when you are trying to become broke.

From Success to Broke Tip #3: Choose Cash over Profit

Cash is what you have sitting in your bank account.

Profit is the net position after you subtract expenses from the income you've made – the report that shows your net profit (or loss) is called an income statement.

Want to make decisions that will ruin your business and potentially ruin you? Be sure to mix-up these two terms all the time.

Successful entrepreneurs look at their income statement when ascertaining whether their business is going well, or if it is suffering. They do not go by what the bank statement reveals, as it is not a real reflection of net profit (or loss). The bank statement may contain incoming cash, which the owner has invested or borrowed to keep the business afloat and there may be payments pending, therefore totally distorting the actual income situation.

If your aim is to make terrible financial decisions, and make sure they are based on incorrect and misleading data, ignore your income statement totally.

Simply whip out your bank statement every time you have a question about the profitability of your business, see that your credit cards aren't maxed out, and go on a spending spree.

You will be sure to hit the rock bottom in no time.

From Success to Broke Tip #4: Always think you know it all:

Simply over evaluate your business idea.

Nothing can accelerate your plunge into the deep, dark depths of failure, debt, and loneliness faster than overinflating your business idea in your head.

Have you ever been told by a trusted advisor, family member, friend or the little voice inside you, that your business idea is exactly that, just an idea? It could either be true, or it could be false. Only you can decide. Have you been told that your idea won't work? That it doesn't have a leg to stand on? That your income forecast seems inflated? That your growth projections appear to be made up? That your cost estimates have no merit? That it looks like you haven't thought about competition, barriers to entry, or ease of losing your market to a giant? And that your business will be cash flow negative for years to come?

If you find yourself in the above situation, be sure to ignore every voice of reason as you charge full throttle, towards the twinkly mirage that is your new business idea.

Do not worry about validating your projections with facts. Believe that everyone who is genuinely trying to help you has just gone crazy. Assure yourself that simply thinking your idea will eventually become a successful business is all you need to succeed. Others are simply jealous of your future "success", or lack of their own.

Make sure never to open your mind to listen to the people who know more than you. Hold firm to your incorrect perceptions. Don't educate yourself or get help. Don't show your business plan to someone who understands the industry, has important statistics/numbers, or can help you with market research. Make sure to have a narrow mindset and totally shut down when someone challenges your theories or assumptions.

Now, sit back and enjoy the free fall.

From Success to Broke Tip #5: Be the Boss!

One of the coolest things about owning your own business is that you don't have a boss! But, what you do have is responsibility.

No more working fixed hours, no one to report to, no deadlines, no more rules to follow, no more waking up at a particular time.

Not having a boss also brings some challenges like:

No more working fixed hours, no one to report to, no deadlines, no more rules to follow, no more waking up at a particular time.

A successful business owner would make sure that just because there's no manager breathing down their necks, they don't stop maintaining discipline. If there are no more rules to follow, they create a framework for themselves, have schedules, keep deadlines, and they hold themselves to the highest standards of organization and integrity — even when no one is watching.

To avoid being successful, assume you have free reign! You are the owner of your business and you do as you plcasc. Micromanage around your subordinates and partners, yet tell everyone that your rules do not apply to you. Sleep in, delay submissions, break promises, always be late, ignore clients you are not comfortable dealing with, don't learn any new skills, miss deadlines, and always remind yourself that you are the king of your universe.

This will help you will lose money, clients, reputation and potentially friends and family.

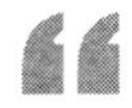

A successful business is a team effort, consisting of the business owner(s), family, friends, the management team, employees, suppliers, bankers, advisors and clients — they are all woven right into the fabric of every business.

You may receive bills from government agencies, partners, and clients, hefty penalties, notices and sanctions. These are all signs that you are magnificently avoiding success and making the downfall of your business permanent with every passing day.

From Success to Broke Tip #6: Have Terrible Communications Skills

A successful business is a team effort, consisting of the business owner(s), family, friends, the management team, employees, suppliers, bankers, advisors and clients — they are all woven right into the fabric of every business. The more diverse they are, and the closer the weave is knit, the more attractive and stronger is its composition.

Make sure to dismantle this fabric, and you can achieve a lasting collapse of your business. The quickest way to achieve this is to alienate your allies.

Successful business owners are polite, humble, kind and forgiving - especially in difficult situations. They face problems with grace and do not become vain when they are victorious.

You however must be tactless, arrogant, and inconsiderate. Slowly but surely you will be left totally alone.

At first, there may be some trusted colleagues, friends and family who just won't leave your side, even with your disrespectful attitude, sense of entitlement and belly-aching, but rest assured, with a perpetual dose of arrogance and thoughtlessness, you will drive them away in no time.

Once you lose the people around you and your team begins to weaken, the downfall of your business is not far away!

Without tact, team, skill and will, you will have what you need to write your destiny. Throw in your lack of grip on your financial numbers and an unsubstantiated business idea and you have a perfect recipe for disaster.

There you go, you just single-handedly ran what could have been a thriving business, right into the ground.

Oh, and if you want to become successful instead, take all the above tips and simply do the exact opposite.

See you at the top!

★★★★★

Cash Is King

Entrepreneurs love everything about business. They talk, breathe and even dream about business in general.

Their own business they love even more.

There are many aspects and segments of a business. Most entrepreneurs are very passionate about several of these aspects - their products, their services, the way they have set up their business - they simply love it.

Then there are segments of the business that they don't like or don't feel equipped to deal with.

One such skill, which in my experience most business owners either don't like or are not very good at, is their numbers. Bookkeeping, accounting, cash flow, taxes, payroll —anything to do with numbers.

It's great being passionate about your business, but without knowing your numbers, having passion is not enough. If you do not know what your numbers are at all times, it could be fatal for your business.

In my role as a business consultant, I often find that entrepreneurs, especially the ones who don't like the numbers, do not understand the difference between profitability and cash flow.

Think about it, do YOU know the difference between the two?

Let's pause here. Before you read the next few lines, ask yourself if you know the difference.

Form an answer in your head and then read the next paragraph to validate your current understanding.

Let me give you an example to explain the difference between the two. Let's say you have a product, for example, you have a pen to sell. The pen costs you $5 (your cost), and you sell the pen for $12 (your selling price). As soon as you sold the pen, you made a profit of seven dollars (your selling price of $12 less your cost of $5 equals $7). Great, your business is profitable. Keep in mind though that although you have a profit, you don't have cash until your customer pays their invoice - this is called cash flow.

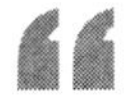

When we analyze business closures or bankruptcies, we often find that most businesses do not go out of business because they lack a profitable product or service, but they go out of business because they don't have adequate cash to pay the bills.

Many business owners do not understand this difference and often find themselves caught off guard, because having a profitable business takes their focus away from the fact that their cash flow position may not that great. Having poor cash flow often leaves them in a difficult position, i.e. they don't have enough cash flow to pay the bills.

When we analyze business closures or bankruptcies, we often find that most businesses do not go out of business because they lack a profitable product or service, but they go out of business because they don't have adequate cash to pay the bills. For this reason, it is extremely important that cash flow is managed wisely — for mere survival of the business.

My number one piece of advice for startups and for entrepreneurs in their initial phase is, this is the best time to reach out for external financing, when a business plan is being made and owners are injecting their own capital, i.e. shareholders' investment into the business.

Keep this in mind, more often than not, banks or any financial institution will only give you financing when you have your own money invested in the business. If you start your business and use all your money first (i.e. initial capital), then decide to go to the bank, it is highly unlikely that the bank will entertain your funding request - certainly not at current commercial terms.

In a nutshell, cash flow is the single most important focus for business survival. So much so, that a business with good cash flow may sustain a period of operations with losses, on the other hand it is not possible to sustain a profitable business with no cash to pay the bills.

Simply put, no cash means no business. So, how can you improve your cash flow?

Here are two key strategies for improved and sustained cash flow:

Strategy 1: Positive Net Payment Terms

A big reason why some businesses have cash flow problems is that their payment terms are very different from their collection terms, i.e. they have negative net payment terms.

Let's take an example of a local business that is working with a large national client for which the collection terms they have agreed to are 60 days. On the flip side, the payment terms which most of the local business's suppliers have allowed is 30 days.

Do you see the problem right there? Any given point in time it takes this business twice the amount of time to collect its money (i.e. 60 days), compared to the time it has to pay its suppliers (i.e. 30 days). This creates a scenario of negative cash flow where the business will always need cash injection for growth.

The right cash flow strategy is where collection terms are 'lower' than the payment terms, which would allow the business to fund itself, and any excess cash flow could be used for business growth.

When a business has attained a position of positive net payment terms, and is operating in such a state for a sustained period of time, investors and financial institutions see this (using cash flow ratios). This is really appreciated by the funding partners as they see this as a testament to the fact that the business owner knows what they are doing, and will also be able to wisely use and manage investor's money.

This makes obtaining financing from investors easy - which is music to an entrepreneur's ears.

Strategy 2: Having twelve to eighteen months of working capital

This strategy is simple, and obvious, but still you would be surprised how many times I come across businesses failing to follow this principle.

So, what is the principle?

When starting a business, prepare a business plan with a thorough financial projection, that includes a cash flow forecast for at least the first three years, and ensure you have enough cash in the business to sustain for the first 12 - 18 months.

Time for a short business story; a few months ago, I met with three friends who recently opened a restaurant. They were referred to me by an existing client, who said, "Please could you talk to these guys? They are very passionate about their restaurant business but need advice about their cash flow".

In my first meeting with these young entrepreneurs, I learned about their story and their journey. They had pooled together a total of $60,000 to start a restaurant. They thought (only thought, as there was no business plan prepared) they had enough money to launch the restaurant and then the business would pay the expenses itself.

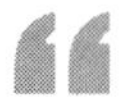

The fact of the matter is that cash is vital for success of all businesses, even not-for-profit ventures and social enterprises - they all need cash. Period.

I explained the reality to them. How the business actually works is that it will take them months, if not years, to be able to reach a point where sales are enough to generate all the required cash flow to be able to pay the bills.

I explained to them that in the first few months and years, they will have working capital needs, cash needed to run the day to day operations of a business.

The right way to do business is to incorporate this initial cash flow shortfall of a few months or even a few years (depending on the industry) into the business plan and reach out to funding partners/investors to get the loan and investment upfront. When you have the money, people will invest in your business. DO NOT wait until you burn all your initial capital and then seek funding / investment, as we mentioned above, once you are out of cash - acquiring funding is a challenge.

Bottom Line:

I can't emphasize enough the importance of cash flow for the sustainability and growth of any business. Think in terms of cash.

Don't believe that it will make you sound like a mean or materialistic entrepreneur who is all about money.

The fact of the matter is that cash is vital for success of all businesses, even not-for-profit ventures and social enterprises - they all need cash. Period.

Do yourself and your business a big favor; plan your cash flow right from the time the business idea starts brewing in your mind. Cash is to the business what oxygen is to you.

★★★★★

Are You a Risk Taker?

In this chapter, we're going to focus on you, your history, and your ability to step out of your comfort zone. Let me begin this chapter with a question, actually two.

Do you ever think about skydiving? You know, jumping out of a plane at around 18,000 feet? Probably not. Or, maybe you're a risk taker at heart but just don't have time.

Are you feeling dizzy just thinking about it?

It's okay if your answer was yes both times. There's a conflict, right? You may think about it but not want to actually do it.

How about going for a hike alone on a trail less travelled? For some, this would make you feel extremely uncomfortable – being alone and away from civilization with the possibility of encountering a beast!

Yet others would probably be packing their camera and bear spray already.

Our feelings about these, or any of our major life decisions, lie in the risk we associate with the event.

So, what is risk? To me, it is what you see when you look out of the window of the box we live in - called our comfort zone.

There are two things about the comfort zone. 1) The door outside is locked shut and it opens only from the inside and 2) although there is word comfort in there, it is more like an I-am-used-to-it zone.

I learned a thing or two about comfort zones and how absolutely barren it is, growing up in a poor family in a third world country where the government provided nothing worth having for free, even if you paid taxes. Water, food, electricity, clean air, health care and education were luxuries. In North America we don't have those same problems. Looking back, I can see how the struggle shaped me, my vision, and my drive for the future.

But for me, those weren't my pain points.

My pain comes from my abusive father. My childhood is tainted with memories of him beating my mother, never holding down a job, stealing what little my mom would save, cheating, and lying. Divorce was taboo. This pathetic life was apparently better than the risk of my mom being on her own with three kids with no support from our family, the legal system, or our government.

This comfort zone offered me no comfort whatsoever.

By my early teens, I had had enough. I stood up to my father and everyone who had been turning a blind eye to our misery, which led to years of agonizing confrontations. This is the way it had to be in order to grow.

There were days I slept with a hammer under my pillow in case he attacked me in my sleep. I was 18 and didn't have a way out.

With perseverance and a ton of will power, that nightmare did eventually end for my family.

This is my message to you. Every nightmare ends. But only if you continue to stand up and resolve to end it.

It left its scars. Let me ask, what scars do you have that you'll carry into your future? Wear them with honor, for the warrior you are.

Unlike most adults, I do not miss my childhood at all.

However, that life gave me some huge lessons which I was able to channel into my personal and professional life, four of which I would like to share with you here. These four lessons are essentially the life cycle of risk taking.

1. Listen when your mind signals discomfort.
Imagine trying to walk with a rock in your shoe. No matter how beautiful the trail is, who is accompanying you, how much you love to stroll or how expensive your shoes are, until you stop to address the rock in your shoe, you will be miserable.

Next time you are in a foul mood, focus. Why are you having a bad day at work, why did you just again pick a fight with your partner, and why did you borrow against your credit card again?

We consciously or subconsciously confuse symptoms with the actual problem so that we can conveniently exempt ourselves from the responsibility of taking action.

> *We consciously or subconsciously confuse symptoms with the actual problem so that we can conveniently exempt ourselves from the responsibility of taking action.*

Remember, the door out of the comfort zone can only be opened from the inside. Once you stop and focus, you will know exactly what the fix is. It may be inconvenient to face and harsh to hear. For example, perhaps you are in the wrong career, or you need to invest more in your relationship, or you need debt restructuring.

But there is no shortcut. It is as if you break a leg but keep on bandaging your arm, hoping the pain in the leg will go away.

The best way I know how to live is to follow your heart. Studies have shown that kids as young as six months can identify good from bad. We are pre-programmed to know the right answer. Tune into your self-awareness and do what is right, not what is convenient.

2. Dissect your fears. It is said that we are born with only two fears. Of heights, and of loud noise.
It is probably so our ancestors wouldn't die falling down a cliff, or

could avoid being eaten by a lion. All other fears are learned.

The fear of leaving an abusive relationship, quitting a dead-end job, starting a new business, pitching your idea to an investor or simply going up to someone new and introducing yourself.

So, think of the two things that scare you the most. Now ask yourself, "What or who put that fear in me?" I can bet, half the time it is a borrowed fear. Once you know it does not belong to you, you will have no problem parting ways with it.

Remember at the beginning when I asked whether you like the idea of sky diving or do you feel dizzy? I also said that it is okay to say yes both times. Why?

Because courage isn't the absence of fear. It is simply the knowledge that fear isn't calling the shots anymore. Fear can be a powerful driver. It doesn't mean you have to be reckless or sky dive. It means that you can still feel the emotions of fear and push through it.

3. Did you watch the movie *Jumanji 2*? The story goes something like this — four students are physically drawn inside a video game and become their avatars. They have to complete tasks and avoid losing lives.

One of the characters is Moose Finbar, a weapons specialist. He mindlessly carries around something. Do you recall what it was? A backpack. Whenever there was a tool their team needed during their journey, he would find it in the backpack.

I like this movie analogy because it couldn't have been truer for me. I found that once you focus on what needs to be done and commit to doing it, the whole universe swings into motion. Whether it is financial resources, education, mentorship, network or the strength to say no, try literally summoning the tool or skill you need. Reach into your backpack and you will be surprised - you always had that in your toolkit.

At 16, I was doing terribly in school. I had no social skills and would hide under the bed if we had guests over.

At 18, I had to quit my dream of going into medicine due to lack of support and financial resources. I became the primary breadwinner for my family, working two jobs and studying at the same time.

I finally got accepted to begin my Bachelors of Commerce degree because it was cheap, and didn't require me to go to a formal school. I started working full time at an entry-level position in an accounting department - at $50 a month.

> *The only thing that is certain is that we will all die and somehow we still wait for one perfect moment to take action – a moment that may never come.*

As I started to slowly progress, I grew tired of the voices of discouragement around me. With no one else to turn to, I decided to follow the path of self-awareness. I learned about my strengths and weaknesses. And then I summoned. I summoned tools, skills, and the resources I needed. As it became clear in my mind what I needed, the tools kept appearing in my backpack when I needed them.

In other words, I learned firsthand that the saying "when the student is ready, the teacher appears" is true.

Fast-forward a decade. I was in the final year of my Cost and Management accountancy degree, which was 100% sponsored by my employer. I had become the first ever female manager in a company where women comprised a mere 7% of the entire workforce. I had married the love of my life and we moved to Dubai. We made a decent living, supported our family and were able to pay for the education of people in our community.

4. I am always astonished when people wait too long. We grossly underestimate the cost of inaction.

The only thing that is certain is that we will all die and somehow we still wait for one perfect moment to take action – a moment that may never come.

As much as planning is key, taking action is of paramount importance.

We will never be able to plan for all possible issues when making a decision. So give yourself a deadline, do your best research, but then jump. You will find what you need as you go along.

My husband and I have taken that plunge three times in a big way. We uprooted ourselves from the comforts of the country of our own birth to go to Dubai. Nine years later we left the cozy, sunny, warm, tax free, high life in Dubai, and moved to the colder climate of Winnipeg, Canada, to start it all over again.

And a little over two years later, we once again left our respective six figure salaries and executive jobs to focus on our own businesses. Today we own multiple award-winning businesses.

I have learned that calculated risk taking, like any other skill, takes practice to master. So, I do it more and more. The steps are:

1. Listen when your mind signals discomfort.

2. Identify and eliminate any borrowed fears.

3. Summon and master skills you need.

4. Take action.

Every decision you make carries some risk. Every step you take in the direction of your dreams takes you further away from where you are - what you are most comfortable with right now. Learn to be OK with that.

So, turn the knob, open the door, and step out of your comfort zone. Prepare to be dazzled by what you are capable of. There's a new life ahead.

Notes:

Notes:

DEREK LOEPP

LIFETIME ENTREPRENEUR AND BUSINESS COACH

Mentoring Start Ups and Seasoned Entrepreneurs to Success

Derek Loepp is a lifetime entrepreneur who acts with passion and purpose in everything he does. He is the co-founder and CEO of the Real Purpose Group of Companies, an organization which focuses on real estate, health/wellness and business consulting. An executive in the financial services industry, with more than eighteen years of leadership experience, Derek oversees Real Purpose Properties, Real Purpose Holdings and Real Purpose | Real Results.

He possesses an in-depth knowledge across many markets and industries with a unique flair for real estate. He is considered a change leader with an incredible ability to influence others while building strong relationships. Boasting a robust and diverse background in sales servicing, process methodology, best practice development, and business consulting, people have described him as a strategic thinker who is innovative, creative, and focused. His expertise lies in the ability to identify, develop, and construct profitable business ventures.

He aspires to travel the world, offering motivational and mentoring opportunities through large-group speaking engagements. There is no problem that Derek can't solve. He is a practical optimist; his problem-solving skills transcend what normal people consider possible.

Ask him how he's doing and he'll say, "I love my life!" Why? Because of what business consulting and real estate has and continues to provide for him. He is fiercely loyal to his family, friends, and business partners. He is deeply in love with his partner in life, love, and business, Jamie, and cherishes the time he spends with their five sons.

★★★★★

What Motivates You?

Most of us travel through life focused on making ourselves and others happy, striving for achievement, making money, and following the path of our dreams.

Through it all, we seldom slow down to ask ourselves *why*.

This book gave me a chance to pause and ask myself that very question. One of the questions I have been asked most often is why I chose to write a book. Life is a hectic whirlwind as it is, with family, business, and activities. Why would anyone take on a project of such magnitude? Less than five percent of humans write a book. It takes time, it's your intellectual property, and it's important. What you write won't just fade away. It will be available forever as a roadmap to others, in print!

My answer to this question has always been tied to my motivations, and they are four-fold.

My very first motivation for taking time to write this book is because of my longing to INFORM. It goes without saying that people simply don't know what they don't know, especially when it comes to entrepreneurship. Almost everybody starts out from a position of ignorance. It is this global ignorance of the principles of success in entrepreneurship that makes self-development extremely critical to every entrepreneur's ultimate success; you can't be a seasoned entrepreneur and not know this. I have gone through several phases of this requisite self-development and it is my ultimate desire to help inform other entrepreneurs of everything I've learned, so they too can have success in business and in their personal lives.

My second motivation for writing this book is to properly EDUCATE others of my generation and beyond. I desire to clearly articulate the wealth of knowledge and experience I have amassed over the years. I also wish to successfully share and communicate this knowledge with other entrepreneurs so that we can perpetuate success. In this way, the growth and sustainability of future generations are guaranteed.

Writing a book is about legacy.

My wife and I have five boys, ages eight to twenty-two, who I am constantly seeking opportunities to educate. How can I make the biggest impact?

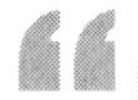

I have always believed that for you to be great, you must be primed, willing and fully ready to take action

I seriously suspect that, secretly, they aren't all too keen on embracing those learning opportunities. But on the flipside, I have been pleasantly rewarded with the most humbling testimonial of all, the testimonial of my eldest son. I can tell that it was quite difficult for him to grasp the principles, practices, and concepts I taught him growing up, but now, my son often comes up to me and says things like, "Dad, I totally get it now. Now, I understand what you were trying to teach me and I really appreciate you taking the time to do that when I was younger." Imagine my joy at hearing that. You see, people are often unaware they lack the proper education required to actualize their deep aspirations, and when they eventually see the light, they appreciate you for being the one who opened their eyes. It is my sincere hope that the body of knowledge and practical information I am sharing in this book will educate everyone out there willing to learn from it, including you.

The third, in my four-fold motivation for writing this book, is my desire to INSPIRE others to be better at whatever it is they are currently doing or have set their sights on. Sometimes, when you educate people, you have merely made them aware, but when you inspire people, you make them want to act, to fly, and to surpass themselves and any obstacle or previous limitation they may have been held back by. It is not enough to know. It is critical to act on whatever it is you do know. While many seek to be better people and to enjoy a better quality of life, most are usually unwilling to proactively pursue their dreams.

I have always believed that for you to be great, you must be primed, willing and fully ready to take action - *focused action.* It is my desire to inspire every single person who reads this book to take action.

My last motivation for writing this book has to do with my desire to EARN. However cliché it may sound, there is a world of truth in the saying that "You can't help other people before helping yourself."

This is a guidebook for the start up or seasoned business owner. Personally, I hope that as you travel through each of the lessons of this book, you will be enriched with knowledge and experience that will ultimately translate into real earning opportunities for you.

★★★★★

Which Pig Are You?

Being an entrepreneur can be confusing. It's up to you to make all of the decisions. How will you grow with your business? How can you grow without compromising your desires and values?

The first advice I have for you is that you must ensure you build and set up your business in such a way that you will grow into it and not grow out of it.

Everyone knows the story of the three little pigs that set out to build their houses with three different materials. The first built with straw, the second built with sticks, and the third built a house made of bricks. It was no surprise to anyone that the big bad wolf was able to blow down the first two houses made of straw and sticks, but was unable to destroy the thirds pig's house made of bricks.

As elementary as this story sounds, the principles taught therein are fundamental and must be grasped by every new business owner, or anyone who is interested in starting a business.

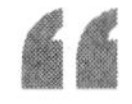

When I started building my business, I was determined and failure wasn't an option. I also knew that success could not be attained just by wishing for it.

During the early stages of my entrepreneurial journey, when I started the Real Purpose Group of Companies, I had a very clear vision in my mind. I had made the conscious choice to succeed, and to do that I had to ensure that what I would be investing my life into something of real importance.

When I started building my business, I was determined and failure wasn't an option. I also knew that success could not be attained just by wishing for it. I had to be accountable to myself. I had to focus on my goals and I had to be efficient in how I spent my time. I also had to be sure that my business was built from the ground up in such a way that it could be scaled well into the future.

In other words, I built my business to grow into it, not to grow out of it. As a business owner and investor, I have met several individuals and groups who start out in business without ever thinking through how they intend to structure their businesses, operations, and processes. They just opened up for business almost arbitrarily; only to find themselves stranded six to twelve months down the road, perhaps even becoming temporarily successful, with many clients, but needing to play catch-up and having to go back to the drawing board, to re-engineer or change almost everything about their business if they intended to survive, or more importantly thrive.

CALL TO ACTION

Allow me to share some action steps with you to help you establish and build your business in such a way that you will be growing into it, and not growing out of it.

Remember, my goal in writing this book is not just to inform or educate you, but to go one step further to inspire you to take action that will translate into tangible, measurable results in your life and business. Here I outline six action steps that I encourage you to take to help you achieve success in your business:

1. Take Time out to Reflect on Your Business Purpose

The first action step you need to take is to reflect deeply on who you are and on what you are doing. If, as of this moment, you either don't have a business yet, or you are just starting out, then it is most likely that you haven't taken any (or most) steps required to set up your business in a sustainable manner. This is essentially just "straw" with which you build your business. That is where I come in.

This is the time for you to reflect on your business goals, at the very beginning. You need to ask yourself why you are in business. As early as possible, you first want to identify your *purpose*, as well as to outline your income goals. Why are you in business? Why this particular business? What problem are you trying to solve? Who are you there to serve? Are you sure your business is needed? Are you in the right place at the right time? What are your goals from an income perspective? What tools do you need to realistically achieve your income goals? Where can you find such tools?

As you can see, this is what the reflection action step is about. Asking, probing, and answering the important questions that will help you to form a robust and sustainable worldview of your own business, the industry in which your business operates, as well as the prevailing business environment within which you are seeking to operate. Do this now, do this early, do this correctly, and you're already beginning to position your business for long-term success.

2. Create a Detailed Plan

Once you have a clear vision, mission, and purpose regarding your business, my next action step is that you must create a detailed plan and framework upon which your entire business

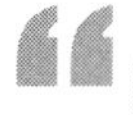

There is no long-term success in business without a practical, credible, and realistic plan

operations will be built. Yes, you are convinced that you should be in business and that your business is needed in the community, now the question is, how do you intend to profit from this business of yours? How are you going to get from A to Z? How are you going to complete all the things you need to complete, structure all you need to structure, design all you need to design, obtain all you need to obtain, etc., to get your business off the ground?

There is no long-term success in business without a practical, credible, and realistic plan; this is why this second step is essential. Your plan should also answer concerns like when do I start? How do I start? What do I need? Where do I start? How can we sustain this once we start? What happens if something goes wrong?

One does not just wish themselves into business; to be successful, you need to create a detailed plan for your business, a plan to define the kind of structure and platform that your business will have and within which it will operate.

3. Build a Capable Team

At this stage in your business, and as early as possible, the next thing you need to do now is to build a capable team. Please read that statement again. I didn't just say you need to build a team, I said you need to build a capable team, a competent team. Your team should consist, not just of friends and cronies who have very little business acumen to bring to the table, rather, you need competent professionals who know what they are doing and are good at doing it.

I am one of the many people who work in a team to ensure the success and long-term sustainability of my business. Just because it is my business, is no reason to do it alone. Let's be realistic, I can't do it alone, because I am not good at everything; no one is. Every entrepreneur must face this truth: you cannot do it all!

Every sustainable business empire has been built and is being sustained by capable teams. Individuals come and go, but the roles within a team remain.

As you begin building a team, it is important that you identify everyone's strengths and weaknesses within the team to ensure you have all the right people doing all the right things.

Team members can either be partners, employees, consultants or independent contractors, but, as I pointed out earlier, you don't build teams based on sentiment, but based on objective contributions they can make to your business and/or the project at hand. You therefore need a checklist of parameters by which you assess the inclusion or exclusion of each individual from your business team.

4. Begin Documenting Your Processes

You now know why you are in business, you have drawn out a solid plan to help you achieve your business objectives, and have set about assembling your dream team. The next action step I have for you is to document your processes. By now, certain operations have already commenced, but even if you are still at the drawing board stage, you can still map out your processes, or the processes you intend to adopt when you eventually start.

You need to begin documenting your processes, and your customer experience. This will help you systematize your business. Begin by detailing your operational processes, how you will position your business, what your customers will experience, how you intend to solve their problems, and how you intend to keep them long-term.

You must know that the successful businesses in today's marketplace are entirely systematized. Flying by the seat of your pants won't cut it any longer, you need to understand and document each process, and you need to understand your customer's experience, map it in advance and enhance it in retrospect.

I will share more about customer experience in a future lesson, but for now just know that it is critical to your long-term success, which is why it must be mapped out in detail.

5. Understand Your Return on Investment (ROI)

The next big step for you now is to get a handle on your ROI. For every dollar you spend or invest in your business, you will need to determine the return on that dollar. ROI is a technical concept used to measure the amount of gain generated or loss incurred on any amount of money, invested over a given period of time. Let's say you intend to spend a hundred dollars in any part of your business. It is your duty to first understand and determine what the return on that hundred dollars will be over a desired period.

While understanding your ROI is of critical importance to your success, both short-term and long-term, I still have a couple words of advice to give you as you consider spending money in your business, and to help you determine your ROI.

The first piece of advice I have for you is, don't be cheap. Always remember that you're building this business to grow into it, so you don't want to be cheap or to penny-pinch.

Anyone who is intent on building a successful and enduring business must understand that it is often necessary to spend a significant amount of money upfront to get going. However, once you start getting traction and start generating cash flow, that money is invariably paid back. In fact, if you can scale properly, you're bound to make that money back exponentially.

My second piece of advice, to help you properly understand and determine your return on investment, is that you must do your research.

The higher the amount of money you're investing into your business, any part of your business, the more the research you will be required to do in order to determine that you're making a solid business decision. You don't want to be sloppy when it comes to doing your research. Not only do you want to evaluate new decisions and investments into your business, but you also want to periodically scrutinize your entire business, to identify those areas where your dollar investments are actually bringing in low or zero return on your investment, in order to stop such situations as early as possible through taking the required actions.

We all know that it is important to monitor and evaluate how you're spending your time and where, but you also need to constantly monitor and evaluate where you're spending money, and keep abreast of your spending to ensure that your investments are always truly adding value to your business as you keep growing into your business.

The higher the amount of money you are investing into your business, the more research you will be required to do.

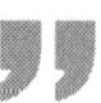

6. Monitor You Results and Performance

The last action step I have for you under this lesson is that you need to closely monitor your results and track your performance. A very wise saying comes to mind here, "the things that get tracked are the things that get done." Meaning, it is not good enough to put a plan in place and to create a business around that plan, you also need to develop the discipline of continuously monitoring and tracking your results to succeed long-term.

Without a proper tracking system or without consciously monitoring your results, you cannot determine whether you're really making money or losing money. Look at the sports industry today for example, analytics are heavily relied upon to assemble teams and develop game day strategies. When running a business, just as in sports, tracking data is essential.

> *it is not good enough to put a plan in place and to create a business around that plan, you also need to develop the discipline of continuously monitoring and tracking your results to succeed long-term*

As you monitor your performance, you must also be constantly re-evaluating and adjusting. Imagine for a moment that you made a decision in your business in its early stages, a decision that worked out quite well over a 12-month period, but taking another look at it now you realize that, that same activity isn't working as it used to, nor is it as effective, what would you do? I'll tell you what I think you need to do. You need to reevaluate; you must pivot. Now you have to look for new triggers, and you have to find new ways to do the same thing or achieve the same results. Another possible outcome is, you may have to come to terms with the fact that perhaps that initiative is no longer an opportunity that your business can profit from in your current market, and perhaps it has outlived its usefulness. Rather than modifying it, you simply need to pull the plug on it entirely.

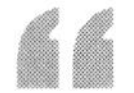

a business that is left unattended is a business that will most certainly die!

Either way, don't be vain, and don't be rigid, because you need to continuously re-evaluate and adjust your business based on variables that change.

Socrates, the famous Greek philosopher and mentor to Plato, once said, "An unexamined life is a life not worth living". In a similar manner, a business that is left unattended is a business that will most certainly die!

SHORT RECAP

I guarantee that conscientiously executing these six action steps in your business will go a long way in helping to position your business as one you can grow into, and not one you will soon outgrow.

You may be asking, "What happens if I don't build my business properly?"

In my opinion, you'll look unprofessional, you'll be susceptible to making costly mistakes, and you'll possibly develop a significantly damaged reputation. As far as building a new business goes, there's an old adage, "You only get one chance to make a good first impression." Word-of-mouth spreads very quickly and bad news often travels faster than good. As quickly as you get into business, you can also be out of business if you don't build it properly.

Consider those who will constitute your clients and consider the types of customers you want to attract; if you don't build your business properly, you'll end up looking unprofessional, constantly make mistakes, and your business could ultimately fold up and flop. I'm sure you don't want this to be your experience in business, so please learn to build properly as early as possible.

Remember that you need to identify your purpose and income goals, you need to create a detailed plan and framework for your business. You need to build a competent and capable team, and you need to document your processes and customer experience. You need to ensure you fully understand your ROI on all your spending, and lastly, you need to monitor your results continuously so that you can always be in a position to constantly reevaluate and adjust as required for long-term success.

MISTAKES TO AVOID

In addition to the action steps I outlined for you, I also include a few common mistakes I want to ensure you avoid when building your business, especially when your desire is to build a business that will endure. Make sure you avoid the following:

1. Lack of Commitment

   Regardless of the particular aspect of life or human relations we are looking at, being committed has always been one of the critical ingredients to success. When it comes to your own personal business, you must ensure that you are fully committed; it is non-negotiable. I can attest that most of the people I've seen fail in business were often people who, in their minds truly desired to succeed like any other, but their bodies and souls weren't just willing to fully commit to the requirements of attaining that success. Wanting to achieve significant success in business without being fully committed to the cause is the result of a wrong mindset. This is why it is critical for you to develop the right mindset prior to venturing into business; the mindset of being fully committed, going all-in, and going all the way.

2. Being Overly Price-sensitive

The second mistake I want to help you avoid is being overly price-sensitive. Remember that I spoke of properly understanding your ROI in one of the preceding lessons, and that you need to make sure you're not spending money in the wrong places, or for the wrong reasons. Yet, understanding your ROI should also not become an excuse for you to become cheap.

You need to strike the balance in order to move your business forward.

For example, if something is going to cost you a thousand dollars and you believe that this price is exorbitant, but upon close examination you see that this thousand-dollar investment will make you ten thousand dollars in profit or earnings, would you still consider this particular investment to be a wise business decision or not?

For me, I would take that ROI any day of the week. Yet, I know there are many people who would rather spend a hundred dollars to make a hundred while trying to play it safe, even though a 0% ROI is not great!

I am not in any way saying that you'll always need to spend more to make more money. However, that is often the case in many businesses, particularly when you have a good idea and you can scale it quickly. What I am saying is that you mustn't be too sensitive about pricing. You will need to invest money to make money. Always focus on the return on investment, not the amount of money you're putting into it in the first place. Let your ROI justify your spending.

3. Procrastination

Thirdly, you must avoid procrastination. Procrastination can be defined as constantly putting off until tomorrow what you ought to be doing today. This bad habit is a killer for any business, no matter what has gone into it. Growing up, especially during my high school years, all the way through university, I could say that I was the most chronic procrastinator ever. There were certain things I simply didn't want to do, I used to convince myself that I could do them in shorter amounts of time and I kept telling myself I'd do them later. That's the mindset of a procrastinator, "I'll do it later." Looking back, I probably missed many opportunities to do some pretty cool and amazing things in those years. Now, I make it a point in my life, a conscious resolution not to procrastinate on anything.

Now, when I get home from work, after dinner with my family, I don't just flop on the couch in front of the TV. Instead, I go into my office and I look for ways to add value to my businesses. I spend time with my family in a way that adds value to our relationship.

Invest in others but also be intentional about investing in yourself. Know that procrastination can absolutely kill your business. If you have decided to build a business, then do it! Don't procrastinate. Make every effort and spend every moment you have to build that business.

4. Settling for Less Than Your Expectation

    The last mistake you should avoid is settling for less than your expectation. Remember when you started out? You set goals, business goals, sales goals and income goals, right? You also identified your purpose or your expectations.

    Your ultimate duty now is to ensure that you are either meeting or exceeding those expectations. Do not settle for less, and if you've been settling for less, stop it! You are doing yourself a world of disservice by wasting all that time, energy, and money you've poured into the business thus far. Make sure this doesn't happen.

    I hope you've gleaned helpful information from this lesson and that it will be beneficial to your business and complementary to your personal success. Before wrapping up this chapter, I want to add one additional thing. If you're going to build your business to grow into it and not grow out of it, and you want to take action with real purpose and achieve next-level results, then my recommendation to you is to hire a business consultant to guide you through these critical activities. It is quite possible for you to go it alone, you could read some books, and you could source information using Google, but if you have a paid proven business consultant, they will be much more beneficial to you as they lead you step by step throughout the process.

When seeking to hire a business consultant, always do your due diligence, ask for references, talk to previous clients to see some of the work a potential consultant has completed, and make sure that they have a detailed plan and structure they're going to take you through.

Choosing to take this step makes you more of a business owner than merely being self-employed. Hiring someone to help you on tasks and activities, that you're potentially not good at, is one of the key traits of successful business owners. Now, you're thinking like a boss, like a businessperson, and you're investing money in your business.

In the next lesson, I am going to share with you one of the biggest and most easily avoidable mistakes new entrepreneurs make when talking to prospects for the first time.

★★★★★

Duh, I Don't Know?

How do you know you're on the right track when it comes to marketing and promotions? It is essential for you to promote your business right from the early stages of development.

The best time to focus on your promotional efforts is while you're establishing your business. In order to effectively promote your business, it is crucial that you have what is now commonly known as an *elevator pitch*. Borrowing a definition from Wikipedia, an elevator pitch is a short description of your idea, product, company, or yourself, in a way that fully captures the entire complex concept such that any listener can understand, within a very short period of time, usually no more than thirty seconds to two minutes.

What's Your Story?

The first step in business marketing is to know who you are.

My own definition of an elevator pitch is that it is a brief sixty-second pitch about you and your company that will generate interest from outside investors and/or clients. Teaching business owners about elevator pitches is one of the topics I am most passionate about because I truly believe that it is such a simple, yet highly effective and profitable activity. The concept seems to be so simple that many new entrepreneurs or business owners miss it altogether. And as a result, several opportunities are lost. Before going into the specifics of an elevator pitch, let me first share a bit of my own story with you about this topic.

When I first started my business, somebody asked me what I did. I remember it like it was yesterday, responding in the most unsophisticated way. It was a bunch of double-talk; I was probably more confused than they were when I was done trying to articulate everything I did. When I later reflected on the encounter, I wasn't even sure if I would've worked with myself after hearing me speak. Sadly, thinking back on those opportunities, there were probably a number of them that I lost before I sat down and constructed an elevator pitch. It boggles my mind that such a simple thing could be so easily missed. So, what did I do?

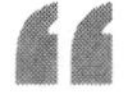

An elevator pitch allows you to establish authority and credibility when engaging with potential clients or prospective investors regarding your business.

I became hungry to improve. I began researching what an elevator pitch was. I studied samples and listened to elevator pitches. I looked for those that lined up with me in terms of what I did in business and then I crafted, edited, tested, and practiced my own elevator pitch. It didn't take me very long from beginning to end, once I identified the need.

Think to yourself how many times you've met somebody at a networking event, a party, or even at work and asked them what they did for a living? Whether you were a prospective client looking to partner or invest, did that person articulate what they did and did they make you want to ask more questions? Think about those times and then think about the times where perhaps you've been asked that same question and how well you managed.

Simply put, the reason an elevator pitch is so important, is because it's your very first impression, your 15 minutes of fame (except it's probably more like 30 to 45 seconds). An elevator pitch allows you to establish authority and credibility when engaging with potential clients or prospective investors regarding your business.

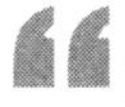

> *a beautifully crafted and effective elevator pitch will help you win clients and investors.*

An elevator pitch is intended to generate enthusiasm and interest about your business. It is particularly important when you're looking for partners. In terms of helping to generate interest in your business, it is quite effective in helping you leave people wanting to know more. When it comes to delivering an elevator pitch, less is more. In today's world, most of us have incredibly short attention spans. Everything has to be immediate and fast, which is what makes an elevator pitch particularly effective in making an unforgettable first impression of yourself and your business. It is a great way to promote your brand, to get people thinking about what you do, and hopefully ask more questions about your business.

One of the major issues I notice when people are working on their elevator pitches, is that people often feel self-conscious talking about their business in glowing terms. We are taught that it's rude to brag about ourselves and it's often hard at the beginning to deliver your elevator pitch with confidence, because you want to be perceived as humble. That's why practicing your elevator pitch until you get over this common discomfort is so important.

You must be wondering how to craft the ideal elevator pitch. I'll be glad to show you. By now, I guess you must have started noticing a theme in my lessons. First, I tell you a little bit about what it is, why it's important, and then we proceed to learning how to apply it. My desire in this book once again is to ensure that you're not just learning the concept, but also learning the practical application. Let's jump into what it takes to construct an elevator pitch.

I have broken down the things you need to do to create your own elevator pitch into short action steps, that you can act on sequentially to arrive at your final destination; a beautifully crafted and effective elevator pitch that will help you win clients and investors.

Step 1: List Your Key Points

The first thing you need to do is to make a comprehensive list of everything you do in your business, as well as why you do each of them. Take a blank sheet of paper and just pour out everything on the page. This isn't the time to worry about sentence structure or grammar; that's not important at this stage.

Right now, just focus on itemizing every fact, quality, or trait about your business. Write down things like what your company does, who your business serves, what your goals are, what you have achieved, what you are issues addressing within your industry, and any interesting or memorable facts about your business that makes you stand out from the rest. Just get it all out on paper. Writing it down in this manner is advantageous because it helps you to remember things you may have actually forgotten about your business offer.

Step 2: Prioritize Your List

Once you've listed everything you can about your business, the next thing you need to do is to label and prioritize each one of the items on your list. This is a ranking system whereby you rank the things you've previously listed about your business, according to your own passion for them, the advantages each has to offer your business organization, and the earning potential of each item or activity on your list. How you prioritize or label your items isn't particularly important here, so I wouldn't worry too much about that. For example, it could be numbered from one through three, or from the most important to least important. Whatever way you choose, make sure you assign a value to each item and that your numbering is consistent throughout. This is important so you can return to evaluate the items and view how they measure up in each one of those categories.

Step 3: Expand on Your Top Three Items

First, you made a list of every detail you could remember about your business, and secondly you were asked to prioritize each of the items on your list according to your passion and the value each adds to your business. Now, the next thing you must do is to select the top three points on your list (based on your passion and value-added scale) and then expand on each of them, fleshing out the what, the why, and the how. That is, what is it? How do you do it? And why is it so important to the consumer?

Step 4: Bringing It All Together

When you are through expanding on your three most important items, the next thing to do is to take those items and insert them into an elevator pitch template or framework. This is the culmination of all the previous steps and is quite simple. The format will include who you are, what you do, how you do it, and why it's so important to your potential client, customer, partner, or investor. Once you've plugged these details into the framework, you can now begin to fine-tune your final piece. This is where you begin to focus on grammar, mechanics, flow, believability, credibility, and language.

You must be careful not to repeat too many of the same words. Craft your elevator pitch like you're writing a short story. Create, edit and revise your pitch as many times as you need to. Have another set of eyes review it for readability and flow. Then you're ready for the last step.

Step 5: Take Your Elevator Pitch Out for a Spin

Once you're through composing your elevator pitch and have perfected your piece, it's time to test it. This is the stage where you begin to practice delivering your elevator pitch to your family, friends, and peers, until it naturally rolls off the tongue. This step is very important because you don't want to appear before would-be investors without being able to deliver your elevator pitch fluently without stuttering or mixing up the details, which would defeat the purpose of coming up with an elevator pitch in the first place. It is only when you're completely comfortable with your pitch that we can say it's time to use it on real people. Until then, continue to practice, test, and refine your pitch. Most likely, you'll find yourself stumbling in certain areas, an indication that you may need to change certain words because they're too hard to say quickly. You might also need to pick up non-verbal cues and feedback, like facial expressions or body language during certain sections of your pitch that you will want to tweak. During this testing phase, you might still discover that your pitch doesn't tell the story properly, or it doesn't build in terms of impact. If this is the case, you'll want to rearrange some items around it, while you keep practicing the presentation. Taking it one-step further, as your business changes course or evolves, and you take on new business activities, you may have to re-evaluate, adjust, and pivot. When this happens, ensure you adjust your elevator pitch to accommodate the changes in your business.

Let's say you finally created a workable elevator pitch. It's tested well and you're comfortable reciting it to other people. Now you are ready. Congratulations, you can now present that elevator pitch that includes all those components, those most impactful qualities when speaking with other people about your business.

A couple of final instructions for you regarding your elevator pitch and its usage:

- Make sure the elements of your elevator pitch form part of your culture, and are incorporated into any products you design; and
- Be sure to consistently use the same message and use it to help you guide your decisions. The reason for this is simple, if you've identified three components that are the most impactful aspects of your business in terms of passion, advantage, and income earning potential, shouldn't they also be your guide as you make decisions regarding your business?

If you do all of these things, you'll have a formal elevator pitch that will allow you to make an unforgettable impression the next time you engage with someone. Ideally, they're going to want to hear more about what you do because of the way you have prepared and articulated where you are in your business.

Conversely, you may be wondering, "What happens if I don't have an elevator pitch? Can it really be that bad?" As I mentioned earlier with my experience before I had an elevator pitch, I was embarrassed and confused, and my listeners probably were too.

I know for a fact that if you don't have an elevator pitch, no one will take you seriously or give you the little time they should to learn about your business. You will look like a rookie without any semblance of professionalism.

More importantly, you'll likely miss some significant income opportunities. This could result in losing somebody who might have actually worked with you, partnered with you, or invested in you. They will walk away and never ask you that follow-up question to determine whether there's an opportunity for you to work together. You'll never grow in your business past a particular fixed level.

The impact of becoming stagnant is huge in any business, regardless of previous successes. The average business owner might actually have a decent business behind-the-scenes, but if they want to take that business to the next level, they have to grow their business. And, the only way to grow your business is by working with new people, new customers, new investors, and new partners. Without an elevator pitch, this is unlikely to happen, and a lack of connections will slow you down in all your activities. I hope I have convinced you that you need an elevator pitch, and I have taught you how you can craft yours in a way that it will capture the essence of your business, and naturally attract new clients.

Common Mistakes:

The first pitfall you need to avoid when coming up with an elevator pitch is giving out too much detail about your business. Remember, the elevator pitch is only the appetizer, you don't want to give them too much information because then it leaves no room for dialogue or questions, right? Therefore, do not include too much detail. Keep it simple.

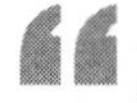

The only time you should be talking after you are done with your pitch, is when responding to a question that you've been asked.

Secondly, you need to avoid being so absorbed with your own presentation that you leave no room for listening. You need to listen. You have to let the elevator pitch speak for itself and at the same time give whoever you are talking to the opportunity to digest your pitch and ask questions. Effective communication is a two-way street. A message has to be passed and received simultaneously. Hence, give your pitch, stop, and then listen. Keep your elevator pitch focused on the audience, and the outcomes, benefits, and results you provide, instead of only focusing on yourself.

The only time you should be talking after you are done with your pitch, is when responding to a question that you've been asked. Lots of people don't like the awkward silences that naturally occur in a conversation, while others are more analytical; often pausing to process the information they received and they need some time to think about what their first question is going to be. Don't try to fill that dead space…just wait. Allow the person you're communicating with to ask a question. Then respond when it's appropriate. You will always learn much more about a person by listening than by talking.

The third common mistake I want you to avoid is making claims or promises you can't keep. Always ensure that you remain authentic and honest. That is why I've taken you through this entire process. I want to make sure you are talking about your business, the advantages of the things you do, the things you're passionate about, and the things you know generate income or have income earning potential.

In essence, don't be a stereotypical salesperson, don't make erroneous income claims; talk about real things, real numbers, and real experiences, because that's what's going to draw somebody in. I'm going to expand upon this in another lesson of this book that will delve a little deeper into the law of attraction.

So, there you have it, three common pitfalls for you to avoid in writing your elevator pitch. If you really want to take *purposeful* action and achieve next-level results with your elevator pitch, I have a couple of result boosters for you.

The first booster is to film or record yourself while presenting your elevator pitch and then critique yourself until you get it perfect. This is where my previous advice of practice, practice, and practice by talking to other people, comes in handy. The most revealing thing you will ever do is film or record and listen to yourself. We can oftentimes be the most critical when it comes to our own work. I can almost guarantee that you're going to hate the way you look and the way you sound, but that's going to force you to look for areas to improve. So, ensure you film and record yourself presenting your elevator pitch so you can critique your performance in real time.

The second booster I want to suggest is that you brand it. You need to incorporate your elevator pitch into your overall brand. Use it often and use it everywhere. This is partly what I was referring to earlier when I told you to integrate it in your business. Put it on your website, your business cards, your auto signature on your email, and your social media platforms. Ensure that it completely infiltrates every aspect of your business, so that when anybody thinks about you, or if somebody mentions you, that is the value that will be associated with your name or image.

Let everyone in your circle know that you act with a *real purpose*, and knowing that everyone who acts with *real purpose* gets *real results*, they'll start expecting the same of you too. Look at me for example; you'll notice all my business names have the same "Real Purpose" phrase in it. We're the Real Purpose Group of Companies.

It's all over our business cards, it's in our auto signatures, it's on our social media platforms, and it's on our website...we have it everywhere. As you broadcast your elevator pitch using diverse promotions, you must ensure that you brand your business with the same language repeatedly, so people will remember you. Once you ensure that your brand and your elevator pitch fully capture what your business is about, and that it is fully featured everywhere within your business, there'll never be a question about what you do in business.

In conclusion, remember to structure your elevator pitch, brand it, take action with real purpose, and then watch how much growth you will achieve in your business. Remember also, that self-development is the key to every entrepreneur's success; you're constantly learning, constantly growing, and constantly improving. Never let the fact that you didn't know about elevator pitches before deter you, now that you've been taught its importance, and you've also been shown how to develop it — it's time to act.

★★★★★

Death of a Sleazy Salesperson

I want you to forget everything you think you know about business, marketing, and sales. Don't worry, you can always pick up and put that stuff back in your head when we are done here, but for right now, clean the slate, listen to the logic of what I am saying... calm the chatter in your head... the worries... and clearly, calmly, understand business in a way you may have never experienced it.

This lesson is not structured like the previous two, because it is in this chapter that I share one of the most fundamental principles that has been critical to my overall business success. Therefore, this chapter will read more like a narrative than like a workbook with tips and action steps. Sleazy usually describes someone or something that is low and nasty, someone who is a cheat or otherwise morally compromised. You definitely don't want to be that person, so beware of developing a sleazy salesperson persona. You don't have to sell, at least not in the way many people think. Let me explain.

When I first started my business, I thought I was going to have to sell, sell, and sell. I believed I was going to have to sell my business to potential investors, sell my skills and abilities to people who wanted to partner with me, and that I was going to have to use my sales skills to find clients. Fortunately for me, I have always been very committed to my personal development and education, which is why I began to educate myself, and eventually discovered the law of attraction.

Broadly defined, the law of attraction could be described as the innate capacity that everyone possesses to attract to our lives anything it is that we happen to be focusing on; an ability that is not in any way limited by race, age, religious beliefs or by gender differences. This law runs on the premise that things within our universe have a tendency of moving towards other similar things, and I am merely using the word 'things' because the law holds true for everything from thoughts and feelings to real objects and people. How it relates directly to you is that the power existing in your mind is used to translate anything your thoughts are particularly focused on, into physical or material reality. As the saying goes, "all thoughts eventually turn into things."

> *Understanding the law of attraction allowed me to stop trying so hard and let my success emanate from me through my interactions, with no ulterior motives.*

Many people talk about this in different ways. Many of the concepts I will address here were originally shared by Don R. Campbell, an authority on real estate investing, particularly in Canada. In fact, some of my points in this chapter have been interpreted from his book and paraphrased here. When I first started reading about the law of attraction, I didn't believe it for a second. What on earth were we trying to attract?

The theory seemed like a bunch of fluff people who were already successful would talk about. It wasn't the law of attraction that made them successful, but now that they have acquired wealth and have become well known, everyone is attracted to them. These people continued to become more successful and wealthier as they built their businesses.

However, at some point, I decided to trust in those who came before me and began doing lots of research. Even though I thought this whole law of attraction thing was garbage, I committed myself to learning how it worked. And work it did. I can't make it any simpler than that. Let me tell you about how it helped me in my business. Understanding the law of attraction allowed me to stop trying so hard and let my success emanate from me through my interactions, with no ulterior motives.

Shortly afterwards, I began learning how to attract clients and return business just by being my authentic and genuine self. I don't mean manufacturing my authenticity, but by being who I was and sharing, not selling. Don R. Campbell refers to it as, "telling not selling." I talk about sharing, not selling, as I interpret and adopt this technique in my business. So, this is not about being a sleazy, used car salesperson. It's not about being someone who uses psychological tricks to get people to say yes to what they are offering, but rather someone who is genuinely excited and enthusiastic about what they do and leaves people just simply wanting to learn more. Why is it so important that you focus on the law of attraction over traditional sales techniques?

The answer is simple, there are too many people selling things. Way too many. Every time you open up Facebook or Instagram, or walk into a store, somebody's always trying to sell you something. So, if you can take a different approach and you can differentiate yourself from everyone else in the same line of business, who do you think they're going to pick? Furthermore, selling using the law of attraction, or better building your business using the law of attraction is far less work and achieves far better results because the types of relationships you tend to develop are longer term. They are not focused on the transaction, but are focused on the experience over time. Additionally, it is easier to sell when you have what they need, and they're coming to you because it's their decision, not yours. So, you're not coming into the relationship in a way where you're trying to convince them that they need what you have and you're not coming across in a way that suggests that you need them more than they need you.

You need to believe that you are able to provide this value and you need to act as if it's already happened.

You are putting yourself in a position of authority; people are going to start coming to you because they're going to be attracted to your success; and that's a fact. They're going to be attracted to how you are different from others, and they're going to be attracted truthfully by all the other long-lasting relationships you've established.

I'm sure a few questions may be running through your mind right now, such as, "Well, how do you attract or sell using the law of attraction? How do you build your business using the law of attraction?" We've already talked about a few things. You've got to set your business up right and have systems, relationships, and follow-through. Don R. Campbell's approach suggests you're not supposed to sell, you're supposed to tell. It is essential that you focus on abundance. You need to believe that you are able to provide this value and you need to act as if it's already happened. That level of confidence will be seen in a way that gives others confidence in you, what you are able to achieve, and deliver to them.

Therefore, focus on abundance, deliver more than expected, and believe that it's already happened; and remember that you also need to be creative. Some of the most successful business owners I know are people who (and I hate to use this cliché term) think outside the box. Think outside the box, circle, triangle, rectangle, parallelogram...whatever structured shape that limits your thinking and confidence, think outside of it all. Because I believe, particularly in business, if you can dream it, and it's legal, it can be done.

Be decisive. People think I am decisive but not analytical enough because of how quickly I make decisions. I'd like to point out how wrong a perception that is, I'm just a "fast-analytic." Decision-making has to be fast so you do not miss out on business opportunities. At the same time, you need to analyze thoroughly before making a decision. Remember you will learn much more by listening than you will by talking. Make sure that as you're speaking with somebody, you're not overbearing or monopolizing the conversation. Truly listen to what motivates them and what they like about what you can offer. Lastly, give back.

Earlier I talked a little bit about my motivation, which is to inform, to educate, to inspire and to earn. I'd like to expand on that now.

I have to earn in order to be able to inform, educate, and inspire. In doing all those things, I'm giving back. People are attracted to other people who give back to their communities, whether it is with business, personal communities or circles where they network. Make sure this is a component of everything you do. This is how you leverage the law of attraction when building your business.

What happens if you don't used the laws of attraction when building your business? Well, it's going to be very difficult to scale your business, because you're just going to run out of people to talk to. Once they get a whiff of your sales pitch, if it comes across as sleazy or self-serving, they're going to stop communicating with you. Period. Clients and leads will just dry up. It's going to be difficult to acquire new customers beyond your inner circle. And it is likely you will never see a referral from an existing client, because they see you as a self-servicing salesperson that does not really care about the client's needs. Some will even be looking to stop doing business with you.

Referrals are often cited as one of the number one drivers of exponential growth in a business. This differentiates people who are simply successful from those that are elite. They work entirely on building their business using referrals.

Once you've established a solid customer base and you are delivering on everything you promised to deliver in those relationships, it's just natural that you're going to attract referrals from your existing clients. If you don't deliver the service and quality you promised, you are going to have a tough time trying to find referrals from your existing clientele. You need to believe in each step that I have just discussed. You need to believe in setting up your business right, sharing not telling, in abundance, and you've got to believe that it's already happened. Be creative, be decisive, listen well, and make sure you give back.

If you want to take action with Real Purpose and achieve next-level results, you need to continuously feed your brain and never stop learning. It is a continuous process and it will help you learn new techniques you can adopt in your business. Also, seek out events and activities where you know your ideal clients spend their time. Network your tail off and make genuine connections. Spending time with prospective clients, even though you may not walk away with a sale in that moment, establishes the groundwork for a future relationship to develop. Remember, I talked earlier about return on investment in your business, well this is your time investment, so understand what that is and track it. Make sure to follow up with prospective individuals and give them another opportunity to spend some time with you, to get to know you and understand why they should be attracted to you and your business.

If you're not doing these things, or if you come off as fake, you will fail. Get your mind right and believe in these things before you start. Manage your experience. Don't come off as something bigger than you are. I talked about how being authentic is something that's very important. People don't need you to be bigger than you are; they just need you to be you, because if you're being you, they know they can trust you. Once you've established a relationship built on trust, you can demonstrate to them why it's the right decision to work with you. Don't be tempted to cut corners and leave a step out. You need every bit of quality to leverage the law of attraction in your business.

Now that you've attracted a prospect, in the next lesson, I shall be discussing with you the specific techniques you can employ to qualify them as clients.

★★★★★

No, I Will Not Work With You!

When I first started out in business, my primary business strategy for acquiring clients was meeting everybody face-to-face. I thought it was the right thing to do. Those days, I would spend countless hours with the wrong people who had no value to add to my business, at the expense of the quality time I could've been enjoying with my family, and money that could've have been better invested. I was so naïve; I would be out buying coffees, lunches or dinners for every person who reached out to me as a potential prospect. Fortunately, I had a friend and an ally like no other in my lovely wife, Jamie, my partner in life, love, and business. One day, she challenged me to do it differently because she saw how rundown I was and how disappointed I was with the results of my efforts. I would call her on the way back home from these coffee meetings or lunch meetings and complain about wasting an hour and a half or more of my time. I could have been doing so many other things. I had to find a better way to manage my time and ensure I was only meeting with the highest quality potential prospects.

It was at this point my passion for self-development once again kicked in and I set out to do what any successful business owner would do, the same thing you have already done by picking up this book, and that was research. I asked others who were successful how they managed their time when trying to meet with prospects, clients and partners. I needed to know how they knew they had found the right person to spend time with. And guess what? Virtually everyone I spoke to or met with, came back with the same response, a practical question: "What are you doing to qualify your leads?" Qualify my leads? Up until the time I started my research I didn't even know what that was; that's how green I was in business.

I had assumed everybody was a lead, which would be a great mindset if your strategy is to keep chasing your tail all the time, hoping for those diamonds in the rough. Taking their advice (which is what I expect you to do with this book); I too developed a qualifying questionnaire I could use via email, phone, or video conference. A questionnaire containing questions that, by their answers, would weed out those who didn't fit, or better yet, highlight those who were a good fit for my business.

THE ART OF DESIGNING A QUALIFYING QUESTIONNAIRE

The major reason why qualifying your prospective clients, investors, and partners is helpful is that it saves you valuable time and money. These are two extremely precious commodities to a businessperson. Imagine the time that is wasted by taking a prospect out for a coffee meeting or lunch meeting that could have been avoided; then consider the additional time that will still be required to build rapport. If you don't build a rapport before you jump straight into business, you run the risk of appearing too pushy with said prospect.

By the time you discuss business, you've already spent an hour and you haven't made it to the point where you need to be. However, if you had taken the time to learn about them using a qualifying questionnaire, by the time you meet with a prospective client, you can jump right into business.

Therefore, in this lesson I am going show you how to design and implement your own qualifying questionnaire to pre-qualify your prospects. A qualifying questionnaire is going to help increase your close ratio and help you find those people who are actually looking for you. It will also help you to establish yourself as a sophisticated businessperson, because you won't meet with somebody, unless they complete the qualifying questionnaire first. It creates an exclusivity that people want.

They see that you only work with certain people and there's a psychology to that. Naturally, people want something that would appear to be out of their reach.

Qualifying questionnaires are excellent predictors of long-term success for prospective business relationships that you can establish upfront. It also performs a screening or filtering function. For instance, let's say you have a lunch meeting with someone and you think they're potentially good clients, partners or investors. Only, somewhere further along in the relationship, you begin to discover certain things about them that you may have been able to learn much earlier on if you had used a qualifying questionnaire. The beauty of qualifying questionnaires is that they allow you to better prepare for face-to-face meetings. You can look for biases in their answers, as well as for potential objections to what it is that you're offering or discussing with them.

You can thereby be ultra-prepared for that meeting and organically move through the conversation in a manner so that potential biases and objections are resolving themselves. So, how do you do it? How do you create a qualifying questionnaire? It's pretty simple, read on.

1. Identify Your Ideal Prospect

The first thing you need to do in formulating an effective questionnaire is to identify your ideal client, partner or investor to be targeted or attracted. This is known as your avatar. An avatar is the graphic representation of the prospect or their alter ego. You need to ask yourself some important questions like, who do you want to sit down with? What are their interests? Detail every aspect and characteristic of that individual. Know inside and out what your ideal client or investor looks like. Write that down on paper so it's right in front of you. Review, prioritize and determine the most important aspects of your avatar. What are your must-haves?

2. Formulate Your Required Questions

Once you have a clear picture of your preferred candidate in mind and on paper, the next step you need to take is to formulate a series of open-ended questions for the respondents filling out your questionnaire. These are well thought out important questions that will in turn require complete, in-depth responses. You want them to give you the exact information you need, so you have to be very thoughtful when designing these questions.

Write them in a way that gets you what you want in terms of the information needed, to help determine whether you in fact want to meet with them face-to-face. Technology can play a major role in accomplishing this task. Find an application that can electronically deliver these questions in a professional manner and includes the ability to track answers and report to you.

Don't create a homegrown spreadsheet or Word document that has questions people have to fill out and send back to you. You want to make it as easy as possible. There's lots of applications and software out there that'll do this for you. They are easy to design and develop. I use 'Type Form' myself. There's a free version and a paid version. Of course, the paid version provides you with better reporting and information analytics, depending on what you're looking for. I use the free version; it's totally adequate for my needs.

3. Test Your Questions and Questionnaire

Finally, with your questionnaire fully crafted and ready to go, the next step for you is to begin to test your questions with a sample audience. Your goal in using this sampling technique is to get quick feedback regarding whether your questionnaire can help you get the answers you're looking for. After filling in the questionnaire, let your sample audience also give you feedback regarding their overall experience with it. Were the questions easy to answer, were they too intrusive, or were they too personal etc.?

The critical point at this stage is to ensure that you are truly getting the types of answers you need. If not, you need to go back and re-work the questions, because, with a live target audience, you will only get one shot at it. If you do this and do it poorly, then you're no further ahead than if you had you met with them in the first place without the questionnaire. So, make sure you get them right. Adjust your original questions based on the feedback and begin implementing immediately. Don't wait. Get it out there and do it right away. Evaluate your results. If you're not getting the information you were looking for, ask yourself why. What could you add to the question to get a better answer? Tweak the questions until you get what you need.

Once you are finished and have incorporated all the things outlined in these three steps, you will have a way of qualifying your prospective clients, investors, and partners.

You're going to start saving time and money by avoiding ill-advised meetings that won't ever pan out. Now may be a good time for you to ask the question, just like in previous chapters, "what happens if you don't implement a qualifying system?'

Well, I've talked about that a bit already from my own personal experience. You're going to have less time to focus on your business, less time to focus on your family, and your business will ultimately suffer because you won't be as involved in your business. And as I said earlier, you're going to end up working with B-list clients. If I have a choice to work with A-list clients or B-list clients, I want A-list clients every time.

If the only thing standing in the way of me working with A-list clients is a qualifying questionnaire or a way to qualify my clients, investors, and partners, what do you think I'm going to do? I'm going to put time and effort there because that is going to save me so much money and time down the road. A qualifying questionnaire will also give me the absolute best clientele to work with.

Before wrapping up this lesson, I also want to caution you about a couple of mistakes to avoid when crafting your own qualifying questionnaire. One of the most common mistakes when putting together your qualifying questionnaire is creating too many questions. You want to get as close to your avatar as possible, but you're not necessarily looking for the perfect client.

If the questionnaire has too many questions, people won't complete it. They'll think you're being too picky and you're going to lose opportunities. You must be strategic when formulating your questions. When you list all the characteristics and the things you want to know about your potential clients, make sure you pick the most powerful ones, the absolute must-haves, the other ones can be worked out later.

The second mistake you need to avoid is being cheap. Don't cheap out, in the long run you can't afford it. I've said this probably twice or thrice already in this book. Don't try to do a homegrown tool or document. You're going to look like a rookie. Remember, you're building a business to grow into it. You're a business owner, so act like one. Either pay for an app or pay for somebody to create one that's branded, this establishes you as an authority in your line of business.

Lastly, you want to avoid being inconsistent in the administration of your qualifying questionnaire. Many business owners end up using their questionnaires inconsistently. They meet somebody and book a meeting right away. They don't follow their process. Processes and systems are what will make you successful. Make sure you follow them consistently. Even if your prospect says it's not for them, insist and revisit it with them. Insist because it's out of respect for their time, energy, and their family. You want to make sure that you are spending valuable time together. And the only way we can do that is by qualifying your clients. You know that this is the only way because you would have already seen the results by doing this. You can establish your authority in that way.

Take action with *real purpose* and achieve those next-level results. Set your qualifier to auto adjudicate the results. I talked about the technology you should purchase. The paid version of an application will often do some auto adjudicating for you. If prospects reach a specific score or you get a specific set of responses, the tool will then automatically send them a scheduling link. In this way, the process is automated and requires very little effort on your part.

So, you've established a qualifying survey of questions, potential clients have answered the questions, those questions come back, and the tool you're using auto adjudicates the answers. If it reaches a certain score, then you'll want to meet with them. The application will automatically send the client a scheduling link. They can schedule a time with you, it pops up on your calendar and there you go. You've set a meeting with a potentially a-list client and you haven't done a single thing, except send them a link to a set of questions. That is real, next-level business planning and it is acting and taking action with *real purpose*.

★★★★★

A GPS for Your Business

You can't go anywhere today without a GPS! The same rule holds true in business, so make sure all your processes and client experiences are mapped. I mentioned in an earlier lesson that I used to be a procrastinator, and I was for quite some time before I became a business owner. Being a procrastinator by nature back then, I had to commit myself to building my business the right way, the first time, and so that I could grow into it, not to grow out of it. I knew that if I didn't act immediately, I would absolutely regret it later. If items aren't written down or tracked, they don't get measured and processes can't be improved. Luckily, owing to my many years in the financial services industry, particularly in an operational area, I'm now a process and efficiency expert.

I already knew the value in ensuring that my processes and my client experiences were mapped out in a very formal way. I knew the value, I knew that I had to invest my time and get it done. For me that was the hardest part. It wasn't that I needed to be convinced that there was value; it was that I just couldn't find the time to do it, despite knowing that there was value in it. I found a template and a process that fit my business and I simply set aside the time and just did it. Not unlike setting time aside to write this book. All this is a process and it takes time. In order to get from

A to Z you need to be committed to it and that's what I did when I first started my business. I mapped both my operational procedures and my end-to-end client experience. The reason those are so important is so that everyone in your business, whether it's a small business or a large business, can see everything the same way. It is standardized for the entire team so that there's absolutely no ambiguity in your operational processes or your client experiences.

“ *When you have the metrics in place to track your conversion rates, you can understand very quickly where a process might have broken down, evaluate why that was the case, and then it gives you an opportunity to fix it.* ”

What it will also do is reduce instances of errors and mistakes. If everyone is on the same page, and understands the way something has to be accomplished, the chances of somebody making a mistake or saying they didn't understand, or they forgot, are far less likely.

Mapping your processes and your client experiences also helps you measure success. When you have the metrics in place to track your conversion rates, you can understand very quickly where a process might have broken down, evaluate why that was the case, and then it gives you an opportunity to fix it. Mapping your processes also eliminates waste and increases efficiency. It minimizes duplication, where you have more than one person doing the same thing. This helps draw those out as you're mapping your processes and client experience, and it will result in a better client experience. Imagine a client experience that's broken or losing leads. You identify the problem and fix it. Now, your leads are coming in more consistently and free of any obstruction.

Mapping your processes also creates accountability within your team. If something happens that is different from the way the process had been designed, you can point to that person or team who didn't follow the processes, and you can hold them accountable. It isn't about pointing fingers, rather, it's about holding people accountable to the processes that everyone has agreed to follow. Now we're getting to the actionable steps, where we ask, how exactly do you map your processes and client experiences? There are many ways to do it and I will be sharing my own process with you. Of course, there are probably some philosophical, theological or other formal models or processes to follow, but I do believe this is a simple and straightforward process that everyone can understand.

1. Identify the Process

First, you need to identify the process you want to map and document. I know that may seem obvious at first, but there's going to be more than one. So, make sure you identify all those processes and experiences you want to document, list them, put them down, and gather as much information about them as possible.

2. Source Adequate Information About Each Process

In relation to gathering as much information as possible about each process, the second step in this sequence is for you to interview those involved with each process, and gather all the details you can about the process. Usually, few people know more about a process than the process performing participants; these are people who have a hand in executing the process and/or are delivering on that process. I believe that the best way to do this is either through direct observations or formal interviews. Learn about their roles in these processes or experiences, and make sure you document them.

3. Determine the Start and End Points of Each Process

You will also want to identify the start and end point of each process, because you're going to have some processes that are dependent on each other; and in some cases, they need to be happening sequentially, while at other times, they need to be happening simultaneously. Knowing when one starts and one ends is critically important to this activity.

4. Break Down Each Process into Distinct Tasks

The next thing you want to do is to break down each process into distinct tasks and decision points. For every operation, there are actions or decisions that need to be made throughout the process and you need to identify where those key actions and decisions exist and place them within the process you're mapping.

5. Create Ownership for Each Unit Task

Each complete process is made up micro tasks with distinct parameters, now you need to create ownership for each of those single points of contact. Each activity and sub-activity must be assigned to specific individuals; everyone needs to fully understand what their roles are. This notification has to be formal.

6. Get A Bird's Eye View of the Entire Process

Next, you need to take a step back and scan each process from end-to-end to determine whether it's an operational process or client experience mapping that you are doing. This is important because their significance is different. For example, operational processes tend to be a little bit more expense or cost-centric, whereas customer experiences tend to be more customer-centric. I believe constantly focusing on the customer in your operational processes and in your client experiences is the key to success. Once you've been able to make these distinctions, try to incorporate technology in your operations as much as possible. I am definitely not telling you to replace all your people with robots, but you can employ technology to the maximum amount you are willing to expend, to enable a process and automate it.

It will save you time, and probably save you money as well. If the person whose job can be better done through technology is still of value to the team, you can move that person into another area of the business. If that person is truly talented, you want them working somewhere where they can continue to add value.

7. Create a Catalog of All Process and Experience Maps

Finally, if you've done all the things outlined above, you need to create a catalog of process maps and client experience maps. These maps must be kept safe and they must continue to influence all of your operations. They are no good if you only follow them once and never look at them again. As things change in your business, and as issues arise or potentially unhappy clients or mistakes happen, you need to go back to your maps and to those processes. Identifying where those issues might have occurred, determining whether it was a problem with the process or the person executing the process; and making changes as you see fit and where it makes sense.

Those are the steps you need to follow. What happens if you don't put these process maps in place, or take time in placing and understanding your client experiences? The short answer is that you'll likely never scale because you'll never be able to be as efficient as you need to be to grow. In addition, you're also going to miss potential customers and opportunities. You'll potentially lose customers when they have a bad experience, and you won't even know why or where it happened.

Here's a worst-case scenario. Let's say there is a part of your sales funnel, perhaps your client experience, that's totally broken. You have people coming in via one part of your business through your sales funnel, and there's a part of that sales funnel that's broken, and they basically end up in Never Never Land. Well, you wouldn't even know that you're losing them. If using sales funnels was your only way for clients to gain access to you, it would be obvious that you're losing clients, but if you have multiple ways that clients can engage and get into your business; if one of them is broken and you don't know it, you are losing out on probably tens or hundreds of thousands of dollars in client opportunities.

Having a good client experience that's mapped will help you understand whether they're working properly. If they aren't, it can result in a damaged brand and as I mentioned earlier, if you don't have these processes in place, how do you hold your staff or your team accountable? Consequently, every mistake that happens in your business is now your fault, and you need to take responsibility for it rather than understanding where it might have broken down.

COMMON MISTAKES

When you're mapping your processes and your client experiences, there are some common mistakes I want you to avoid:

- Don't be too general in your process mapping. Being detailed is the best way to do this because you can always take things out later, but you can often never add them back in. So, don't be too general in the steps. You need details to make sure you've got everything covered.

- Another common mistake is having one person looking after all your client processes. This person will be uninspired and not pay attention, as they'd end up leaving all the processes in the hands of the performing team. You need to have the mapped processes reviewed by many people. Fresh eyes will uncover some of the most revealing things. I know when I've been looking at something too long, my brain is ready to shut off and it's not observing things that I would see if I was looking at it for the first time. I'll give it to a trusted colleague or someone else I can depend on to review closely, and have them look for any mistakes I may have missed. Be sure that once you've got the process maps completed, you're reviewing with many people and getting their feedback.
- The other thing I imagine most people don't do regularly, thus making it another common mistake, is not reviewing their processes regularly. This is not a once-and-done activity. It's ongoing, whether annual, semi-annual, or whenever there's an incident that's occurred in your business that should alert you to look at these processes. When these things happen, you can adjust and improve to avoid similar situations in the future.

Now, if you want to take action with *real purpose*, and achieve those next level results I've been talking about at the end of each of my lessons, here is where you need to put a mechanism in place for your staff to provide real-time feedback. Allow them to take ownership of their ideas, to improve the customer experience or the operational process. This is key. When you receive feedback, you must act immediately. This creates a sense of ownership. Give people a way to be able to provide that real-time feedback and reward them for doing so. The reward doesn't have to be money or a gift. You could show appreciation through praise or other forms of recognition. The best way to reward somebody in your team for providing real-time feedback is by taking ownership, and improving your business through acting on it right away. That shows them you value their opinion and their input. That is the next level tip, act with *real purpose*. In this day and age, you cannot get anywhere without a GPS when you're travelling. The same can be said for business. Make sure your processes and your client experiences are mapped in a way that you know exactly where your business is going and how well it's running.

I hope that I have fulfilled my promise to you, in writing these chapters. With the information I've provided you are now empowered to qualify leads, attract the right people into your business, and document processes. I hope you have been informed, educated, and inspired on how to build a business that will experience enduring and long-term success. One that you will grow into, and not grow out of.

Notes:

Notes:

JONATHAN LIPSON

CANADA'S PREMIER WEALTH COACH

Jonathan has built a life exploring what other people told him NOT to do. Whether it was acting, singing, writing, employment, or business, the majority of his activities up to now have been met with massive opposition. Jonathan responded to this with furious determination and unwavering stubbornness. Sometimes that's what it takes. Now he owns five thriving businesses: a kitchen company; a marketing company helping small businesses; a real estate investment firm, showing people how to increase their returns, and a financial services company providing free education and recommendations to people who want to achieve their dreams. The greatest value to him is showing others how to discover and realize their potential. As a coach, there is nothing more rewarding than helping his students and partners succeed.

★★★★★

★★★★★

Passion = Success

When I think about the beginning of my journey, it always comes back to food. I was a very picky eater as a kid, I ate the same breakfast every day. For nearly 15 years, I ate a bagel and cream cheese for breakfast. I loved Kraft Dinner and chicken fingers at other meals. Frankly, there was little else that was acceptable to me.

As I grew older, I maintained a slightly expanded, clearly defined set of tastes. I watched cooking shows every day looking for ideas, trying to solve what I considered to be the problem: most food tasted awful. But there had to be something I could do about it.

One day I stumbled upon Chef Michael Smith's show and his secret recipe, "Find an ingredient that fires your imagination. Choose other flavors to match. Find the best way to cook it. My secret recipe? Cooking, without a recipe!"

Eureka! His voiceover states that at the beginning of every *Chef At Home* episode. Sometimes inspiration comes from the strangest places and this moment on the 'idiot box' changed everything for me (that's what I lovingly call television, and my reasoning for that is a bit complicated, but more on that later). NOW I knew what I needed to do to make things taste right, I had to invent that taste myself! From that day to this one, I experimented wildly with my spice rack and the contents of my refrigerator. I read cookbooks, blogs and articles online about all these interesting food ideas and I'm still trying to make them all. Did you know that if you walk into a grocery store or restaurant today and find a dish you could happily eat for years at a time, learning to cook it at home is as easy as searching "Simple ____ Recipe" online? The world we live in is incredible.

As I began moving forward in life, I found myself following this secret recipe even outside the kitchen. My first business happened by accident. There was a poster on a bulletin board in my high school. I never took a picture of it; I have a different perspective than most folks with cell phones, who take pictures of everything. But, I found a poster from New York that looks just like the one from my high school (below).

To this day, I have no clue how they posted it in my school. I was actually looking for a job, something part-time and hourly that I could use to earn a little money while I figured out what I wanted to do with my life. Pay attention to this type of thinking too, even at 15 I thought of a job as a means to an end. I intended to use my first job as a springboard to something else, something greater, and at that point in my life I wasn't even aware that there WAS something greater out there. I thought earning my own money and buying my own car was the rich life. I tore a tab off this poster, called the number, and soon after arranged an interview with the manager.

I don't even remember the interview, what I remember was the fight I had with my mother, because I had to buy a sales kit. It had four knives in it, a vegetable peeler, a sharpener, a cutting board, and it made complete sense to me. How could someone buy anything from me if I had nothing to show them? What was the big deal? I was persuasive, she wrote me a check, and I paid for the kit.

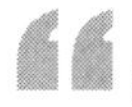

Making my passion profitable had never occurred to me before, but it's something that stands out when you look at a lot of very successful businesses

I was still naïve enough that I didn't realize I truly didn't have a job, I was actually starting my first business. I had become a network marketer. But for me, this followed the secret recipe. My job was to sit and talk with people, make some snacks (to show off my wares), and sell them the tools to make the same stuff. Plus, we got to eat the snacks. I thought it was genius! Now, not only could I figure out ways to make delicious food, but I could get paid for it too.

Making my passion profitable had never occurred to me before, but it's something that stands out when you look at a lot of very successful businesses. A significant percentage of startups are created by people who are frustrated by a problem, which they dwell on, and solve. It is impossible not to be passionate about it after all that time and effort, and surely the problem solver is not alone in their suffering, so they find ways to deliver their solution.

When their problem is widespread, their solution is simple, easily implemented, and they come up with an effective distribution strategy, their business tends to be successful for a long time.

My favorite example of this has always been the market. By this I mean, the actual, physical market that used to exist in the days of the horse and carriage, the place people would go to buy food and other wares. The problem back then for farmers was, once the fruits and vegetables and grains were grown, how could they bring in customers to buy them? Sure, many locals and neighbors would know about the harvest and might come to trade, but what about people farther away? The market solved this problem. It was widely advertised, scheduled regularly, many people participated and brought their close group of contacts. Whatever goods were brought to be sold would often be purchased by happy customers.

I adapted the secret recipe to my business. Being passionate about kitchen knives doesn't come easily, but as I challenged myself to find recipes, I found my passion grew. And who doesn't like eating? It wasn't long before my passion began turning into sales. Finding the best recipes became a game I played with my customers, we chose alternative flavors that matched. We literally found the best way to cook them, et voila ... success was mine.

The other reason my passion was so vital, was because of all the garbage I was able to ignore because of it. Business is a very difficult activity, both physically and mentally.

When you have a clear purpose in mind and you believe in it, nothing else matters, that is what the secret recipe did for me, and I believe that is what it does for everyone. Each of us has our own secret recipe; we just have to discover it. And cook it, of course.

The reason I share this as my first lesson is because it is important as a foundation for the future. The reason you'll do what you do is what becomes the seed that grows the entire forest of your business. You'll probably hear at some point in your career "farming" is a better business strategy than "hunting and gathering", but, however you grow your business, you'll need basic motivation.

How motivated are you? Are you passionate on a daily basis or burnt out? The first summer I opened my business I had a massive commitment to make for a 15 year-old. I had to pay hundreds of dollars, drive to Edmonton, and stay three days for a sales conference. Remember how I convinced my mother that allowing me to try this was a good idea? Well going to a conference at 15, with a group of people she didn't know, in someone else's car, without my mother looking over my shoulder, did not go over well.

I did it though, and easily too. The arrangements were made, I booked a hotel room, drove down with some of my team, folks who knew how to plan a road trip, since I'd never been on one before. That might have had something to do with my mother's reservations (oh well). I had complete confidence that my plan would work. And why wouldn't it? I knew exactly what I was going there to do, I would learn from the best people in our company about exactly how to sell kitchen equipment. They would teach me marketing and sales methods much more effective than what I knew. I would come home, go back to work with twice the skill, and achieve success.

Failure didn't occur to me, not even after the conference was over, when we were getting set to go and our driver hit another car in the parking lot. Her vehicle was no longer roadworthy. No one was hurt thankfully, and as we exited the vehicle, all of us were in shock. I did the only thing I could think of.

Our national sales manager had given us his phone number in case we ever needed help, and he was a very successful man. I called him and explained what happened, and he came down to the parking lot right away. He guided us through the process of getting a tow, made sure we were all right, and booked us rooms for an extra night. Thank goodness the repair could be done quickly, but I STILL don't know what it cost him to help us, because he paid for it all.

There are plenty of people who would have taken this setback, finances and time wasted, and used it as an excuse to quit. Not one of the people I travelled with had that idea, we were all too focused on what we aimed to accomplish. You will encounter obstacles. Are you committed to overcoming them?

Our goals, our dreams, all of it stemmed from a belief in our business, including what and who we were doing it for. Our secret recipes, they kept us going. We were having too good a time to stop now!

★★★★★

The Winners Mindset: Indomitable Will

Each one of the entrepreneurs have made it here with their own will, dreams, goals, habits and stories of success. Right now you may be motivated, wanting to rush out and hit the ground running. I want to congratulate you for making it this far, because most people don't. In fact, did you know almost a third of high school graduates never read another book after graduation? Over 40% of university graduates never read another book. Yet reading one hour per day in your chosen field will make you an international expert in seven years.

Thank you for staying with us and for having the commitment to remain dedicated to your own personal growth. Many people jump ahead in life, skip the learning process, and end up learning the hard way. That might sound like a day in the life of an entrepreneur, but it is also true that we can all learn from each other. This book is dedicated to you because each one of us has taken time from busy schedules to create this entrepreneurial guide-book for you.

The reason I point this out is because I want you to understand, right now, that you are doing something extraordinary. It may not feel like it, but you are.

Taking action in your inner world is just as important as taking action in your external world. Maybe even more important. Today you are taking the time to learn.

Just reading this book is part of what I call the winners mindset. I would define the winners' mindset, as "doing things which most people refuse to do, that you know will lead to success." Most people consider such acts to be extraordinary, and tell tales of the people who did them. In the old days we used the word heroes, and now it's meshed with celebrity or influencer, but the meaning hasn't changed much. So how can you continually develop and maintain a winner's mindset? How can you be your own hero? I'm not talking about one big action. It's a series of small and intensive commitments you'll take to get there. Reading this book shows that you're dedicated to winning. You're investing in yourself, so that you may also pay it forward and invest in others.

I personally learn from books, videos, and other humans, but also from musicals. I took lessons from Broadway, from playwrights and scripts, and wonderful musical numbers. I'm talking about the shows *Annie*, *Fiddler on the Roof*, *Oliver Twist*, *The Music Man,* and *The Wizard of Oz*. All are classic musicals, and I believe they contain important lessons. I'm also a fan of them because as a young boy I was a stage actor in reproductions of them.

I was eight years old when I starred in my first musical reproduction, and the show was *Oliver Twist*. My parents never took it too seriously, but I loved to sing and dance and I would repeat lines of movies and television shows verbatim. It seemed an obvious choice to start in theatre as many legendary people have started there. I had and still have dreams of success in that area, but what I noticed as I studied my lines, was that the characters in these plays had a strong cerebral quality about them. Now some folks will be quick to point out, negatively, that I was studying fiction and those same people would suggest my time would be better spent on other things. I always ask them in return, where else can I find pure ideals, other than fiction? And then I'd carry on my merry way, sharpening my mind with every page I read. Imagination is a great element of life. We can create magic with imagination. We can envision products or businesses that never existed before, with imagination.

In every great legend, and every story that inspired followers and re-telling that I could ever find, the characters had strong convictions, which they never strayed from. I began to ask myself how that could be.

If victory was that simple, how could I become such a person? I learned that when your purpose is clear, and your strategy sound, there's not much that can get in your way.

The challenges that remain once you've tackled all your physical obstacles are simply mental ones. Now, I say "simply mental" as if you could just think them away. YOU CAN. But they rarely seem so easily conquered. You may have experienced this in your own life.

When I was 12 and 13 years old, I was bullied terribly. I suffered intense personal pain, every day, and no matter who I told, or how I tried to get help, there was none there for me. In those days, children were hanging themselves in my community because the bullying was so bad, and I believe the problem persists today because of the same deficits in our education. I thought a lot about ending my pain in a similar fashion to what I'd heard on the news. I was so angry and hurt, all the time. I wanted it to stop. In the midst of making my final plans, I had an epiphany.

I was allowing this to happen.

The thought froze me in my tracks as I considered it. Think of it with me: When someone says or does something that hurts you, whether physically, mentally, emotionally, or otherwise... you are taking part in the experience, are you not? Your choices have power. And you can choose something else. You can choose what to DO about it.

There are some people who will read this page and dismiss it as fluffy garbage. But, more powerful minds will seize the influence of that idea and realize that they too, hold the power of thought in their minds. We all have it! This is what I touched on before, when I said you could overcome negativity. Just the way you are manifesting a situation into a reality affects your power in real life.

The general idea I'm getting at, is that developing a winners mindset involves being mentally strong or mentally tough. There's a fantastic book on mental toughness, appropriately titled *177 Mental Toughness Secrets of the World Class*, that I recommend to anyone even thinking of entering into business. It is the start of a journey that will redefine what you think you're capable of, and quite probably change your future. I challenge you to submerge yourself in developing a winner's mindset. I hope you enjoy the ride.

Realizing my power over bullies came to me long before I'd ever heard of mental toughness. I didn't even understand the concept. But what I thought was, "Why the heck do I care what these losers think and say and do? What would Oliver Twist have done in my shoes? What would Dorothy do?" These characters participated in their own stories, just as I was doing in my life. When they were threatened, they were in far greater danger than I was. The wicked witch wanted to destroy Dorothy! The evil Mr. Bumble wanted Oliver to work to his death! And there I was, worrying about what 12 and 13-year-old kids thought of me? Insanity! It was so stupid, and a primary part of my identity, what I believe about myself, is that I am not stupid. Therefore, I had to choose what I would do next.

Realizing the insignificance of what I considered to be big problems only moments ago, I made plans. I also got extremely angry, with myself, with the other kids who made me feel so badly, with the adults who wouldn't help me, and it led to a confrontation with the person who led the bullying. It's interesting to me, thinking back, that I happened to channel my anger toward a single focus, instead of trying to spread it out. I considered the sources of my problems, and dealt with them directly. First, my weak mind. Then, my strongest bully. On and on, I charged at my problems with a rage that never ended, until I developed a reputation as a brutal little boy.

I was actually sent to anger management classes and referred to a guidance counselor regularly during that time. I enjoyed these experiences immensely, because these were people who truly listened to me. I sailed through my days no longer troubled by bullies or incompetent adults. In less than a week, my life turned completely around.

> *Your will must be indomitable*
> *for you to succeed. Believe that.*

What most people will say when they see someone single-mindedly pursuing their goals, is to slow down. Take it easy. Stop and smell the roses. Don't work too hard. Don't hurt yourself. That kind of distraction has destroyed many people's dreams, and continues to do so. There is no substitute for intense, focused, hard work; if you want something, YOU MUST GO GET IT. To be successful, you'll have to hear, see, feel, and ignore a lot of criticism.

If you're as big of a fan of wordplay and reading as I am, you might have heard the word indomitable before. Determined, stubborn, unconquerable, these are all part of the concept, but none of them individually has quite the same substance as indomitable. Icebergs are indomitable. Time is indomitable. Your will must be indomitable for you to succeed. Believe that.

I did, and no matter what pain I experienced, I continued to believe that I would master it. I knew that obstacles would fall before me and that there was no other alternative but to be indomitable. Yes, I am on some kind of power trip, the kind that comes from Knowing I Am Capable and I Will Succeed. And I want you to feel that too. You are capable. You will succeed. When you begin to feel that self-doubt creep in, remind yourself. You've already achieved so much. You've got this!

Combine your winners' mindset with your indomitable will, and you've solved 90% of the puzzle. The other 10% is simply taking action, which, if you spend as much time thinking about how to solve a problem as I do, it will be a cinch.

Let's get back to the indomitable iceberg for a second. Why are icebergs indomitable? Imagine standing in front of thousands of pounds of water, snow, and ice as it is slowly coming toward you. What would you do, keep standing there? Uh, no. You're an intelligent life form, your instincts are programmed for survival, and you would hightail it away from the danger.

Now flip the scenario, you ARE the iceberg. What are your concerns? None. You're an iceberg. Aside from the fact that icebergs are inanimate, even if you were some sort of science fiction experiment, imagine yourself as a living iceberg. You would not be concerned at all about things on the ground, you would simply crush them as you move inevitably forward. Make that your mindset. Say it out loud: I AM AN ICEBERG.

Once you develop mental toughness and a winner's mindset, it's time to begin focusing on your relationships with others. You got this!

★★★★★

Networking: Building Relationships

As you read this book it's our expectation that you will learn, grow, and use these principles in your own life. We are here for you and even if we never actually meet face to face, know that we've traveled this road too. You cannot do it alone.

No person is an island, and it is nearly impossible to accomplish great things alone. It takes a great team, a group that's focused on the same goal. The great feats in the world from the pyramids to Stonehenge to the Rockefeller Center were accomplished not by one man acting alone, but through one vision and many hands building it. So how do you build a team? How do you find people to work with?

Today, networking is both simple and intimidating. On one hand, people are more interconnected than ever before. No matter what business you're in, with social media, cell phones, and video-conferencing, there is no excuse not to talk with people. On the other hand, the act of conversing with people, reading body language, building and maintaining relationships, are all skills that are rarely taught outside of the business community. This chapter is far too short to get into the finer details of networking, but we can cover the broad aspects.

First of all, the definition of networking is simple. It is a socioeconomic activity by which business people and entrepreneurs meet to:

- Form business relationships
- Share information
- Seek potential partners for ventures
- Recognize, create, or act upon business opportunities

This is what you can expect when meeting other people. Networking is not the same as prospecting. Rather, the goal of networking is to expand the circle of people you as a business owner can draw upon, to create opportunities and participate in projects with. You never know what will come from networking and relationship building.

When all of the authors met to discuss this book, we discovered we had a mutual passion for teaching and sharing our stories. Every one of us wanted to share and help others grow. It didn't matter that each one of us had different goals and dreams. We all knew that networking was an activity that was necessary to grow and move closer to our desired outcomes.

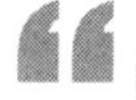

Think of your avatar as the profile of the person you most want to work with. Who are they? What do they look like? What is their skillset? What are their problems, and how can you solve those problems?

Now that you understand the activity, the question becomes, where do you go to network? Thankfully, this is easy, as there are all kinds of groups that advertise themselves as networking centers. Business networking groups exist in every country; networking is not a new phenomenon. About the only thing that's changed in the last few decades is that the groups can reach across oceans and time zones with ease, making business simpler than ever before.

While locating places to network is simpler now, a rather important question is, who should you network with? How do you determine this? My solution has always been to create an avatar. Think of your avatar as the profile of the person you most want to work with. Who are they? What do they look like? What is their skillset? What are their problems, and how can you solve those problems? When you find the answers to these questions, you'll be ready to take action.

Once you find the groups and people who are your ideal partners, how do you talk to them? One of my favorite networking tools is the acronym F.O.R.D., which stands for Family, Occupation, Recreation, Dream. Whether you're meeting someone for the first time, or the fifth time, an easy way to develop familiarity with them is to ask them about these four areas. Becoming a smooth communicator is key, so read books and listen to professional audio content that details the process. There are many successful people such as Brian Tracy, Bob Proctor, Ed Mylett, Grant Cardone, Barbara Corcoran, and Arlene Dickinson, who freely and willingly share a trove of brilliant content about networking and marketing. The book *How to Win Friends and Influence People* by Dale Carnegie, is a staple in the business community. Read it, discuss the ideas with your community, and you'll soon find people who align with your vision. As a bonus, it's not bad to develop your own methods at the same time. You'll learn from others as you talk to them and those people will help you make more connections. The cycle is a potentially limitless funnel of value once you begin.

“ *What does it really take to start a relationship? Not much. An introduction, practice in the mirror, and a firm handshake.*

Remember, more important than talking to others is listening to what they have to say, and finding points of alignment. People like to be around others who think the same way they do. We tend to be attracted to and trust those who talk like us, act like us, and think like us. Don't be afraid to mimic someone a little bit, if you like something about them. It will actually build more value in your relationship.

What does it really take to start a relationship? Not much. An introduction, practice in the mirror, and a firm handshake. Make eye contact with the person. What does it take to maintain a relationship? That is where the real value is. Consider the fact that on average, half of all salespeople never approach someone more than once to do business together. How does that seem like a successful approach? But when they put in the effort to build a relationship, the numbers go up. Eighty percent of sales are made between the fifth and twelfth meetings, and the only way to see someone that often is to develop a relationship.

What is a relationship? It is simply an exchange of value. If I help you, how likely is it that you will help me in return? Great empires have been forged on this simple principle. What relationship will increase the value of your business, your sales volume, your efficiency, and your market share? Again, draw this out. Find out who you need to talk to, what they do, and what value you bring them, which will result in them working with you. It helps if you share some interests outside of business, but it's not necessary.

The last part of networking is the simplest, but most crucial part. Without this one piece, the relationship may fail to produce your ideal results. What I'm talking about is following up.

Not only do you need to find common ground, develop that exchange of value, and be grateful for the concerted power, but you need to maintain that relationship. Doing this serves two purposes: first, it builds your reputation. Whether you maintain a relationship or not, it sends a message to all those associated with you and your connections, about how you conduct business. The image you present will matter in your future endeavors ALWAYS. So, you need to develop a system of how you'll handle the relationship going forward.

There are many tools available to do this, from auto-responders and email services, to personal assistants and other staff. You'll want to take charge of the most important connections to your business yourself, but the best entrepreneurs find ways to transform the time commitment from these relationships into something that can be mutually beneficial. Have you ever heard the idea that more deals are done on the golf course than in the boardroom? The meaning behind it is simple and yet profound: many people enjoy playing golf and so they structure their closing meeting on the course, in the clubhouse over dinner, or wherever it's convenient around their hobby.

The power of this cannot be over-estimated: it provides recreation, is good for business, provides a tax deduction, and strengthens the relationship between the players. It even creates an excuse to follow-up, because you can schedule the next game! The social dynamics are terrific. You should also read Derek's lesson about developing powerful yet authentic elevator pitches. We all need to understand how to communicate well with the people we meet.

Now let's see if you can be a professional networker. Imagine you're talking with a prospect and they ask you these questions. Practice the art of networking:

What is it about what you do, or what you want to do, that makes you so excited? Keep it simple, something that I can be excited about too. What is it?

____

____

____

What is it about your project, product, or service that is easy to believe in? What is difficult to believe in?

____

____

____

Action!

Thinking is good, doing is better. At the end of all your planning, the most important thing related to your business is taking action.

Execute! Try your plan out. See how you perform. This is not a short race, but a marathon that can last years before you create a working, sustainable business. In the beginning, I encourage people to treat their business like a corporate job. My reasoning is simple: jobs have set hours, parameters, and processes to follow. Anyone can be trained to do a job given enough time and mentorship, and it is that simplicity that makes a corporate structure so powerful in the business world.

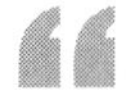

Thinking is good, doing is better. At the end of all your planning, the most important thing related to your business is taking action.

When most people start a business, they begin as a one-person operation. Maybe if you are lucky, your spouse, best friend, or a family member joins you in your venture. But whether you have some help in the beginning or not, the discipline I spoke of earlier is far easier to maintain if you convince yourself at first that you are working for someone else.

It is quite the emotional split; on one hand, I crave the freedom and success that comes from owning my work. On the other hand, I value the discipline that comes with being accountable to another party. The bridge I reached in my own mind was that I work for my future self. I have clear goals and objectives outlined for each of the businesses I own, and I monitor my progress towards those outcomes with exacting detail. Future me is my CEO, and I am the employee reporting to him.

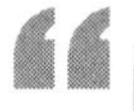

Future me is my CEO, and I am the employee reporting to him.

Having this perspective makes it difficult to fail if you are truly serious about your vision. Even when writing this chapter, I am sure I was not the only person to set goals and deadlines for myself, and monitor my activity in order to reach them. I had to lock myself in a room sometimes to write, away from the distractions around me. I had a job to do.

So how do you take action? For some it is simple. They have a plan and just do it. Others need a push. I will share two of the best perspectives I have ever heard of. The first comes from the book *Eat That Frog*, by Brian Tracy.

I have had the privilege of being mentored by Brian Tracy, perhaps one of the foremost business guides in the world. One guideline he lives by, is that you must do a difficult thing first, if you are going to make any progress in your day. We all have things we dread, from getting out of bed, to going to work, to coming home. Some are big things, some are small, but we try to avoid them.

Brian's advice, to become a more effective person, is to pick whatever it is that you want to do the least. Find that thing, and make it the first thing you accomplish. Make it part of your affirmations that this will be the first thing you accomplish because you are skilled at it, and because you're capable. Adding this to your daily routine will not only de-sensitize you to the pain of doing things you dislike, but it will build your resistance to those feelings of avoidance altogether. When that happens, you gain that shift in perspective from avoidance to approach, and you become awesomely capable.

The other piece of advice I would give you comes from the book *The 5 Second Rule* by Mel Robbins. Once you've identified your frog, you give yourself five seconds to get started. Simply count backwards from five with the commitment to yourself that you will eat your frog, and you will be amazed at how quickly you shift your behavior. Again, this is not someone else's magic spell that works on you. No, this is a spell you cast on yourself. The change is gradual, but it happens within you.

With any change in ourselves, we must expect an adjustment period. Just as athletes do not turn professional overnight, neither do business people become amazing founders or CEOs just by training their minds and pounding the pavement. They also allow themselves to fail. And oh my, do they fail.

CEOs are probably the best failures in the world. Like Thomas Edison, they simply find many ways to overcome what doesn't work. They keep trying; keep approaching their problems from different angles, with different tools or avenues they hadn't thought of yet.

This is the part of action that makes business so bloody difficult! And frustrating. And time consuming. My goodness, the amount of failures I've had in my own career trying various things would have made most people give up. But you, like me, picked up this book because we won't quit. We are determined.

I think often about one of my favorite fantasy characters from my childhood, a boy with magical powers who, regardless of all his strengths, was unable to move a rock. This was such a simple, stupid problem, it seemed unbelievable that it would plague his character. He failed repeatedly, even burying himself in the ground at one point. He never gave up. He asked for help. He learned about things he never knew. Eventually moving rocks with his mind barely required any thought.

My own struggles were less dramatic, but I needed to learn to achieve results in my financial practice. For more than 15 years I struggled, even to make friends, I barely understood body language, and this made it especially difficult to gain clients. But I reminded myself, if a man can learn to throw a boulder, surely I could learn to do business with people. Somehow, that worked for me. Because other people do this, I too must be capable. I needed to learn from them. Once I learned something, I needed to practice it. It was like those piano lessons I shirked all those years ago came back to haunt me.

I threw myself into situations outside of my comfort zone. One of the easiest ways to make an introverted person feel uncomfortable is to stick them in a room full of seasoned business professionals, experts in negotiation, sales, and wealth building. Those people were my avatars, the people I wanted to work with. I knew they would find value in what I was doing, and I knew they could teach me how to do it even better. More than that, I knew speaking with them would help them as well; they could take value from me and give it back in ways I hadn't yet dreamed of.

It. Was. Excellent. The first day, I searched networking on Facebook and showed up at a luncheon put on by a group I'd never heard of. I couldn't remember the names of people after meeting them, but it's something I'm actively working to improve. The highlight for me was looking for business partners. There, at this luncheon, running the show, was a successful gentleman who'd been in finance for over

40 years. At his right side, a woman who built a million dollar company, sold it, and was a successful mentor to other business owners for many years. I went on to meet other successful founders, leaders and visionaries I didn't know were right there in front of me. They told me what to do and I did it. I don't hunt down expert advice and then ignore it, and I'm sure you won't either.

I went on a spree recently, with the goal of meeting one new millionaire per month. I challenged myself to do it and I held myself accountable. I practiced what I preach; I made sure my passion was high and my mind was ready. I knew my networking skills were strong and I developed a plan to act. I decided to show up or gain entry to every business club, meeting, or conversation among the people I'd identified. I would become an expert on them, what they did, why they did it, and how they did it too. I went mad with activity.

What's your comfort zone? As you're reading this you may be thinking of your own discomfort, and areas of your life in which you need to grow. Once you begin, competing with yourself is a great way to spark and keep your momentum. I just had to get out of my own head.

Another favorite story of mine, is a fantasy epic which describes how magic is simply wanting something, and letting yourself have it. I've always seen business the same way; it's simply the desire to realize some sort of outcome and then building the mechanisms to achieve it. The one thing in business we control is our own activity. With that understanding, the only thing to worry about is — are we doing the right activities?

My last lesson talks about this. For now, the takeaway for you is simple. If you're starting by yourself, then every day you must improve your efforts. Even if it's by the smallest margin, every step forward is a victory.

Up until this page, we have been talking about working alone. Good businesses can be built alone, but great businesses require a team. The sooner you start utilizing the efforts of a team, the sooner you will be able to grow and test your idea. That's partly what my last chapter will be about. I'm introducing it now, because if I'm being honest, there are so many good ideas out in the world, it's truly unbelievable that more people don't become successful business owners. How can this be?

Learning discipline, networking, being utterly committed to what you're doing, and being mentored regarding success, surely that's enough? Only it isn't. The most crucial part of any business is its ability to pivot towards success. Sometimes this means shifting from a failing process to a successful one. Other times, it can mean gaining more profitable efficiencies, sharing resources, or leveraging other successes. Most often though, the most valuable asset in a great business is the capacity of its management to evaluate the progress of the business, test it for any threats, and transform their operations to overcome and adapt to the changing market. More fortunes have been gained and lost by those who develop a golden idea, only to have their great contribution overtaken by something better suited to people's needs when circumstances change. Before we start the next lesson, ask yourself this:

Am I ready to take action on my idea? What will my action be? What is my deadline?

____

____

What will the outcome be?

____

____

★★★★★

Evaluating Progress: Recalibration

Welcome to our last lesson together. The other authors in this book also have a great deal of value to share. They are my friends now, but they were only strangers until I became committed to networking. Remember, iron sharpens iron and you may have to kiss some frogs along the way. The rest of the authors here have the same vision, to share our truths with you.

Before you meet them, let's finish our discussion. Let's make sure the business you build takes on a life of its own; one that you are proud to have created. Are you ready?

As I said before, the most important aspect of any business is its ability to analyze itself and adapt to change. In university, they called it metacognition, which is thinking about thinking, and part of that is the ability to identify what you don't know. In business, we must exercise metacognition and adaptability. The only way to gain these is by constant tracking and evaluation of our results. When they meet or exceed our expectations, we can keep the processes we use. Where we fail to achieve our results, we have to ask ourselves if there is a better way.

Consider the times we live in. Ordering a pizza to be delivered to your home is a convenient solution when you work 14, 16, 18 hours and don't care to cook. Or Chinese food. Or fried chicken.

As a matter of fact, why not make it so that whatever food you want, from any restaurant, could be available to you, the consumer, for a few extra dollars? As a proud cook, I try to make as much as I can in my own kitchen, but now I find my time is often better spent solving bigger problems than what I should eat. I would much rather order from any number of delivery services with a wide variety of options. I wonder if anyone else feels the same as I do.

Or what about transportation? Travel? There was a time when taxis, hotels, and travel agencies worked in concert to provide an easy experience to consumers wanting to expand their horizons. Now there are websites, where with a few clicks, I can choose from a horde of options and customize my experience. These services rely on customer data and trend patterns which they actively review in order to function. Gone are the monopolies that existed before, unless the old guards of industry invested in these new ideas.

I am always amused by the story of Netflix, as I heard it. When looking for some investment, Netflix approached what was at the time a dominant force in the rental movie business. That company turned them down. Multiple times. At that time, the company was the best choice around for rental movies, fondly remembered for its late returns policy and as a wonderful place to help plan a quiet night in.

Netflix didn't let that stop them. They capitalized on solving problems which existed in the rental movie market and grew to be a large success. Those who turned down the opportunity to be part of that success have imploded, or are close to it. And planning that quiet night in has never been easier. Just as these new companies have innovated, so too must our businesses.

The question is, are you looking for the cracks?
The flaws in what's available today?
Are you crafting the solutions for those problems?

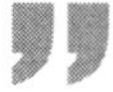

For me, the problem was that most people I knew had old, terrible kitchen knives. They bought the cheap plastic kind from Walmart, and replaced them often. Their pots and pans were scratched up. They were looking for tools that did more than what they currently could. I had the answers. I had the equipment that continues to solve these problems for my customers today. The same goes for my marketing firm. My financial practice. Even my tutoring company, which hasn't had to adapt in nearly a decade, continues to thrive.

The question is, are you looking for the cracks? The flaws in what's available today? Are you crafting the solutions for those problems? Have you been working with insiders and mentors, and have you been developing your own mind to take on your competitors? If you are, what about your own ideas? If you're going to supplant an existing idea, do it simpler, faster, cheaper, or if you're planning on doing more at once, how might you be defeated? How can you improve upon yourself?

Your team will help you with this. It's just like writing a paper for school. Eventually you've reread it so many times your eyes conjure the words you wish to see, rather than see the ones in front of you. For the same reason we ask other people to proofread our work, we ask others to help us innovate and advance. What if someone adds to your already brilliant idea? What if they give you that missing puzzle piece that you've always needed?

One problem that I examined in depth exists in the financial industry today. Many people who are 50+ years old are struggling. I thought to myself, how can this be? They've had years to build a life for themselves and there are so many opportunities out there. Forget whatever mental blocks or false perceptions one might have, we can earn a living simply through sheer effort. So why would anyone find this to be a challenge?

I discovered what I believe to be the flaw, which is miseducation. It's part of the reason I wanted to be a co-author of this book;

to show you that success is more than possible. With the right planning and groundwork, it is probable. With the right connections and mindset, it is likely. And, as long as you remain open-minded, and you evaluate your progress, it is definite.

With regard to finance, many people are not being taught the basic information they need, or worse, they're being taught incorrectly. For example, did you ever learn about credit cards in school? Or investments? Taxes perhaps? What about building wealth and the myriad ways you can do that?

There are millions of people teaching millions more of their children incorrect information about financial literacy.

Forget business, forget employment, for just a moment remember your original goals and dreams and evaluate your progress towards them. Where are you? How much farther do you have to go and what is your vehicle to make it to your destination? How do you calculate these things? For many people, money is involved. Money is not the most important thing, but it is similar to oxygen in that to thrive here, we need it. It's a valuable tool.

If we don't learn correctly about money even though money is integral to our success in so many areas, how can we possibly be successful? Then it hit me. Not only is this affecting older generations, but they're passing down what they know. The problem is generational. Systemic. There are millions of people teaching millions more of their children incorrect information about financial literacy. People are being set up to fail, and they don't know about it.

I re-evaluated everything I had learned up until that point and I saw a clear problem, one that most people are simply too busy to consider. Who has the time to think about making more money when they're struggling to pay off debt? Who worries about their retirement when they're struggling to pay their bills on time every month? Who considers the system they're working in when they're busy managing kids, a mortgage, a marriage, friendships, parents, a career, and anything else that comes up? It's no wonder people are struggling.

What can be done? I searched for an answer, overthinking it. Eventually it was pointed out to me that the knowledge was still available, you just had to learn where to look. But how could I help others with this? Here is where everything clicked.

1. It's never about the money, but what someone can achieve with it.

One of my first mentors told me, "Money is a magnifier. It makes you more of who you already are. If you're a good person without money, you'll be a great one with money. If you're a mean person without money you'll be a terrible person when you've got money."

Never has something been so true in my life. We all know one or more of those cruel people. They have a great life and yet they expend their efforts in causing pain for others. And yet, we can all think of someone equally or more successful, and they seem to be dead set on making things better in the world. Personally, I prefer the second one for company.

2. Since the information seems difficult to access, how can I make sure people get it?

I'll become an educator. I already love to talk; I enjoy spending time with people and bringing them value. I'll build a system of distribution where anyone can access what I know and use it to put themselves in a better position.

3. What about me? I need to eat. I can't teach on an empty stomach.

The financial industry is the highest paying industry in the world. There is nothing people are more focused on than caring for their families, achieving success, creating safety and security for themselves and their loved ones.

I spent so much time working in one niche or another, when the issue I was really attacking was right in front of me. I recalibrated. I looked at what I knew. And I pivoted. I took all of my experience, my customer service and communications training, my mathematical skills, my psychological education, sales ability, everything I knew, and changed how I used it. And I realized that's what I'd been doing for years. From childcare, to food services, to call center work and volunteering at food banks, all the singing and dancing I'd done in musicals and all of my education in schools plus every job I'd ever had. I took all of it and asked, "What is the most effective way I can use this today?"

This is what every business needs to do to remain relevant. This is why so many businesses fail. This is why so many people give up. When you master the ability to recalibrate, to change your view and adapt to new circumstances, you'll find that you fit in anywhere. You can try anything once. Some things you'll be good at, some things you won't. Finding success comes much easier when you can take what you know and apply it however you need to.

I've given you a lot to digest here. Take my advice one-step at a time, but apply consistent daily effort. Always do the hardest task first and use the five-second rule when approaching these tasks. Become a master networker by attending events and practicing. Most of all, be willing to pivot, recalibrate, and adapt when necessary.

Notes:

Notes:

KEVIN KOZAKEWICH

PHYSICAL BRANDING EXPERT

With the goal of creating local jobs, Kevin had one focus on his mind, helping local business owners develop stronger relationships with their clients. In preparation for this, he took the time to specialize in various industries such as eCommerce, importation, retail storefronts, trade shows, and wholesale distribution, finally entering the physical branding industry, where his talents can best serve those around him.

His brand, NORTHERN EXIBITS – A Physical Branding Agency, currently works with over 35,000 North American businesses, providing clients withimmediate, valuable advice, and access to the newest, most impactful physical branding to date.

In addition, Kevin is able to help businesses with their brand presence, scalability, and sustainable growth, with a focus on automation, innovation, community growth, and business to business (B2B) ventures.

Outside of business, Kevin believes that real mentorship should be accessible to those who need it, provided by real business owners who have already built a successful business themselves. This motivated Kevin to start several initiatives: bringing together successful business owners from various demographics to write this book, hosting free monthly entrepreneurial events, with the goal of helping new and existing entrepreneurs connect and work together towards mutual success.

★★★★★

Four Steps to Build a Sustainable Business

Starting a business is one of the most difficult adventures anyone can commit to. What often starts out as a passion- filled activity, quickly leads to a heavy commitment that pays less than minimum wage.

As an entrepreneur, you're already very different from most people. Odds are the music you like isn't from the top 40 latest hits, and the art you enjoy isn't widely valued in the same way you appreciate it. Your interests are part of a niche market where what worked today won't work tomorrow.

It's easy to believe we can start a business simply from our greatest passions and a will to succeed. If we choose to pursue it, we can work 80 hours per week and create something incredible, pushing ourselves harder than anyone else we know, only to fail in the end. Why?

We all hope to achieve independence or financial freedom. We wake up every morning, chanting the same motivational quotes, talking day and night about our vision to friends and family, pouring our heart and soul into everything we do, only to fail and be left with nothing, except a very valuable learning experience.

Throughout our journey, the more we fail, the more our passion fades. Long hours cause us to be forever fatigued. Struggles cause our constant smiles to become constant frowns. That bright, motivated entrepreneur everyone once knew, transformed from someone with a big heart and big dreams, into a quiet, reserved, defeated pessimist.

Regardless of all the reasons we can come up with about why this happens, there's one reason that trumps all others; it's too easy to create a business which simply isn't sustainable.

> *If you don't sell customers exactly what they want, where they want, and how they want it, they will shop somewhere else, and there's always a competitor waiting to take your place.*

You see, we're sold this concept called the entrepreneurial dream, where we are told all we need to do to start our own business is to find something we're passionate about, then hustle and grind 80 hours per week for a few years. And somehow, our business will then magically become successful.

We're frequently sold this concept in schools, books, franchises, places that earn money from entrepreneurial services, and businesses who want you to sell their stuff. It's one of the biggest lies that exists today, making everyone believe that owning a business is easy, that anyone can do it, and if it doesn't work, it's simply because you didn't try hard enough, or lacked motivation.

Yet what's so powerful about this myth is, most entrepreneurs realize quickly that what they're doing isn't working, but because they've invested so much time and energy into their business, they become inflexible, regularly hiding their failures from their colleagues. They can't fathom giving up everything they've been fighting for.

After all, they've spent their entire life fighting. It's one of the only things they've taught themselves to do. To be the underdog and fight against all odds. To convince themselves that success is only a few weeks away.

If you tell them everything they've been fighting for is a lie, and they need to re-start from scratch, it's easier for them to dismiss you, rather than stop what they're doing, abandon what they've built, re-evaluate themselves and everything they stand for in the process.

However, you're different. You chose to read this book. That makes you an extremely rare individual. You know tomorrow is going to bring new challenges, and by reading this book you're preparing yourself for them. It's people like you who change the world. We wrote this book specifically to help people like you.

So, what advice would change the above business owner's lives forever?

Being passionate about what you do is important, but if you want to build a sustainable business that leaves a legacy, there are certain things you need beyond passion. Without them, you might as well quit right now.

The first step to building a sustainable business is understanding that the world by nature is a cruel and unforgiving place. It doesn't care about your dreams, ideals, or what products and services you're passionate about. It doesn't care how much effort you've put in, or how you're going to make the world a better place.

If you don't sell customers exactly what they want, where they want, and how they want it, they will shop somewhere else, and there's always a competitor waiting to take your place.

Imagine a successful grocery chain owned by a vegetarian. You assume their stores only sell vegetarian products. However, the most successful vegetarian owned grocery chains today realized their ideals alone weren't enough to convince a population to change their belief systems, and so were barely able to keep their doors open.

> *If a business isn't making money, it's losing money.*

Instead of accepting defeat, they realized the only way they could create change in the world was by selling customers exactly what they wanted, animal products, but differently.

To them, animal products were the enemy, but if society was hooked on them, they needed to provide customers with both options, along with proper education.

They helped customers make informed decisions by offering tons of valuable information, lined grocery shelves with plenty of vegetarian alternatives, and even made sure the animal products they sold were raised as ethically as possible.

No one can force change upon the world, but we can all be part of the process by helping customers make informed decisions, while offering a pressure-free environment.

The second step in building a sustainable business is that it needs to be profitable. You would think this would be self-explanatory.

If a business isn't making money, it's losing money.

When people decide what their business should sell, they either decide based on their passions, or are opportunists who compare buy and sell prices, believing they can undercut the market to make a profit, forgetting to factor in the cost of monthly business expenses, salaried staff, and their own time.

Many people start a business but hate talking about sales or profit. They see sales as a method to leach money out of other people's pockets, for products or services they don't need. After all, the only way to gain a dollar is to take it from someone else.

Unfortunately, everything in the world can be exploited. Your hands can help people up or push them down.

It's important to believe in the products or services you're offering, and focus on helping other people. The only thing that separates ethical and unethical businesses is whether they give more value to their customers than they take.

Ironically, even non-profit businesses need a sales team and a focus on creating profit. Not only is it needed to help them grow and assist more people, but also so that they can eventually hire a team to replace the founder, creating a legacy.

So, how does one create a profitable business?

To make sure your business is profitable, it's important to create and follow strict budgets.

Imagine if your expenses were so low you only had to make one sale per month to pay off your monthly bills. However, while spending an extra $40 per month doesn't seem like much, it quickly adds up to $480 per year, requiring you to budget at least an extra $1,000 per year in sales, simply to maintain.

This is why it's so important to cut costs wherever you can. Nearly everything you're paying for has a lower cost (if not free) alternative, requiring only a couple of extra hours of your time to research. This knowledge will be a resource for the rest of your life.

It's also very tempting to invest in new products or services before we even have paying clients. While the newest toys are always the most tempting, they also become quickly outdated, losing half their retail value each year.

Instead of investing in every new product or service you see, find clients who are willing to pre-pay, and offer a refund if they receive a sub-standard product. Once you have your client's interest, not only will they help subsidize your new products or services, they will also help you sell more through referrals and valuable testimonials.

As entrepreneurs, it is surprising to discover consumers are often completely uninterested in products we believe to be game changers. Finding paying clients in advance helps us vet whether our products or services are actually viable.

When it comes to creating a budget with enough sales to produce a profit, we also need to ask yourselves a very important, yet difficult question.

"How much am I worth?"

It's too easy to undervalue ourselves, especially when every market has a competitor who offers their services below minimum wage, often out of desperation.

However, if we want to hire capable staff to eventually replace ourselves, we'll have to make sure the wage we charge for our services can support them.

So, how much should a capable staff member earn?

While hundreds of people may line up for a minimum wage job, the best employees know what they're worth and won't stick around for long if they feel undervalued. At the same time, salary isn't the only thing staff are looking for. For the same reasons you quit your job to start your own business, your staff desire their independence too.

Giving them the freedom to choose how and when they work will mean the world to them, as long as their progress can be measured along the way. Set-up their roles like they own their own business and the right people will take full ownership. Once the appropriate people are hired, all you need to do is give staff full accountability by putting the proper systems in place.

It's also important to make sure your products are profitable enough to support a sales team. When working with your sales team to calculate weekly, monthly, or quarterly sales goals, they might realize your goals for them are unattainable and leave. This happens specifically with businesses that focus on one-time non-repeat sales, especially when certain times of the year are slower than others. To keep your talented staff on board long-term, it's important to offer a product or service that generates profit year round through some kind of re-occurring sale, or residual income to help boost your staff's morale.

If sales staff earn upfront commission on each client they secure, plus a re-occurring commission while the client remains with the company, they will now be financially motivated to make your company their priority, and go out of their way to turn a dissatisfied client into a satisfied client.

The third step to building a sustainable business is to focus on helping other businesses succeed, saving them time, money, and energy.

If you can help other businesses help their clients, you can perform much larger transactions in a fraction of the time it would take to sell each product or service individually.

When selling directly to businesses, it isn't difficult to sell $1,000 per month per client. While $1,000 seems like a lot, it's what most companies pay their staff in half a month.

What if you could help a company gain as many clients as one of their sales people, but with guaranteed results and no management? Or how about saving every staff member just one hour each, which results in half a month's worth of time saved? You can also save them money on things they regularly buy, whether that's wholesaling, rent, software, vehicles, advertising, or even branding.

If your sales staff can gain at least one new long-term client every second week, with each client spending $1,000/mo., within five years they'll have gained 130+ clients with an annual revenue of $1,560,000/year. Earning just a 10% commission, they're walking away with an annual salary of $156,000/year.

Taking it a step further, what if your staff could retire by transferring clients to their children through an intergenerational franchise? Now that's creating a legacy.

Finally, the fourth and last step to building a sustainable business is understanding that we tend to push ourselves to achieve more than we're humanly capable of.

As we continuously push ourselves beyond a healthy limit, we tend to lose composure, become fatigued, fall behind on deadlines, neglect very important parts of our lives and — when reality doesn't match our expectations, we break. It's crazy how many successful businesses shutdown because their owners put themselves in a position which demanded more than they could handle.

When we're pushed beyond our limits, our instincts start to kick in. Our fantasies, our cravings, our desires. Eventually, the only place we want to be is anywhere but here. We close our businesses, liquidate everything, cut ties with everyone, and decide it's time to give ourselves a fresh start, often chasing the very independence and freedom we just deprived ourselves of, albeit in a more self-destructive manner.

Some business owners project their stress onto the products or services they're selling and are perfectly happy simply switching business models, building their new business with the same bricks that collapsed the last one. Others idealize the concept of travelling to another city and starting fresh, only to realize they've isolated themselves from their loved ones, while real relationships takes years to form. Those remaining often fall victim to their addictions, hoping to ease their pain, only to suffer when the effects wear off.

The thing is, when a business is profitable enough to hire a team to support you, you shouldn't have to take on more commitments than necessary. If you aren't yet at the point where you can hire staff, it's possible your business is actually a hobby, and that's okay. However, it's important to align your expectations with reality. Remember it takes a team to change the world, and you won't retire from your business without one.

Instead of hiring staff members, you'll likely gain better value from acquiring a business partner first. Someone who can help invest capital, has connections, the right mindset, and inspires both of you to succeed.

Finding your ideal business partner is a lot like finding a life partner. By joining together in business, you'll have to spend a lot of time together and frequently compromise. However, if you ever want to separate, it can quickly become an ugly, expensive legal process no one wants to be a part of.

Not sure where to find the ideal business partner? Attend events, help local leaders, work together to foster community growth, learn how to make your own movements, and eventually you'll meet like-minded people along the way.

Many people post about their businesses online in an attempt to draw in the ideal business partner, but the only people you'll find are those overly eager to be part of the next big thing, who become quickly bored, or those who want to attach themselves to you in an attempt to suck you dry.

Ideal business owners however, have their own dreams and are taking constant, consistent action to achieve them. You'll have to go out and find them, but if you have the chance to work with these action takers, progress can be made very quickly, but hopefully not too hastily for stable growth.

The only way to find an ideal partner with the same values is to search for them. Always become friends with potential business partners for one year before mentioning any proposition to them, to learn who they really are. Sometimes the greatest sales people are just that, sales people. Investigate their actual achievements instead of just their words.

One common mistake people make when searching for a business partner is to search for someone who's exactly like them. However, you need to find someone who's your opposite, but with the same goal and values in mind. If your passion is sales, you likely will need someone who is deliberate and detail oriented to run the back end of the operation. You need a partner whose weaknesses are the opposite of your strengths, and whose strengths supplement your weaknesses. With such differences, there will be many disagreements. Both of you need patience, respect, understanding, a willingness to learn and admit being wrong, but more importantly, boundaries of who makes the final decisions in which areas, and a written list of each other's roles and responsibilities.

Remember that no one is perfect. Humanity arrived at where we are today in the shortest amount of time possible. We're as imperfect as we could possibly be, even after evolving physically and mentally. It took a few highly intelligent people to invent amazing things like electricity, the internet, and wireless radio towers, which magically connect devices in everyone's pockets through light waves. Yet even these few gifted people have their own flaws.

They say most inventors are daydreamers who find it difficult to ever take action.

While the average person can quickly answer a question based on what they already know, inventors answer questions by looking at every conceivable option, sometimes spending days researching and mapping out every conclusion before they make up their minds, unable to focus on anything else in the process.

As annoying as it is for them, they often solve complex problems simply by spending the time to dig just a little deeper than anyone else, thus finding solutions that no one else would.

Ironically, these few clever inventors are often introverts, tired of over-thinking, wishing they could live the lives of those who simply live for today and enjoy the moment. Meanwhile, those who live for today wish they were smarter and able to become deep thinkers, not realizing the freedoms they would give up in the process.

Everyone's different and no one can do everything. This is why most businesses have front-end and back-end staff. Everyone has their own passions and specializations. Not everyone is an effective salesperson, just as not everyone wants an office job. However, by hiring diverse demographics to strengthen each area, you can create a powerful dream team that will work much more reliably than simply hiring a dozen sales people with no one to support them.

Now that we've reached the end of the lesson, do you remember the four steps to building a sustainable business?

1. The world is a cruel and unforgiving place, which doesn't care about what you want. While you can't force your change upon the world, you can be part of the process.

2. You need to focus on building a profitable business. Make monthly budgets and stay on track. Keep expenses low and sell products or services only if clients are willing to pay for them ahead of time. Work with a diverse team to create dream jobs.

3. Focus on helping businesses help their clients. Create a product or service that brings in some kind of re-occurring income.

4. Don't overwork yourself. Business is a long-term game and we need to put the proper systems in place to ensure our own emotional stability. Find a partner whose strengths counteract your weaknesses, much like your dream team should compensate for each other's weaknesses.

Now let's tie it all together in one simple sentence.

To build a sustainable business, you must become profitable enough to afford your dream team. It's only when you have your dream team in place that you can eventually retire if you choose.

Finally, take it slow. We're all alive longer than we think. It's better to take things slow and do everything right the first time, than to rush, and ruin our reputation in the process.

As powerful as this lesson is, there's still much more a business owner needs to know to survive. I believe in you. May these next four lessons help you take your business to the next level, on your path to building a sustainable business.

★★★★★

How I Got Banned from eBay

Instead of telling you how to be successful, I'd rather share my entrepreneurial journey with you so you can learn with me. As someone who has spent the majority of their journey importing and selling products, I'm frequently asked whether eCommerce is a viable business path. I get questions about my experience with importation and wholesale as well. I hope this gives you a glimpse into a diverse and unique industry, which undergoes drastic changes every year.

In 2013, I began to learn the subtle art of importation. From negotiating with overseas suppliers, to ordering $10,000+ shipments from people I'd never met before. Back then, I saw importation as the easiest path to becoming rich. Importation was simple in theory, I've always ordered everything I needed online, and was never taught the importance of shopping local until a much later date.

Before Amazon was a thing, I ordered from eBay all the time and never understood why people thought it was so complicated. After all, I would look for suppliers who had 200+ ratings with a 4+ star average. When I paid for the order, I assumed the supplier in China was a large factory, which would manufacture, then ship the products. Finally, I simply needed to wait two to three months for delivery. If there were any issues, everything was guaranteed by

PayPal. Little did I know, the reality was not that simple.

I didn't realize until much later that many of these Chinese suppliers were small family-owned businesses. Many decided that their best chance at success was to open an online business, take international orders, source materials locally, assemble the products themselves (with the help of their families), and hope each order arrived safely at their destination.

They would then fight online to be the lowest cost supplier, with the hope of doing business with the western world, even if it meant having their family work for free, simply so they could use the profit to put food on the household table, believing one day they'd buy their own freedom.

With next to no profit, these shops had to work fast to get orders shipped as quickly as possible. This sometimes caused them to miss a step or two, which among their customers created the perception of "China quality." Although these products could easily be fixed, most of their western customers believed that their orders had to be absolutely perfect, otherwise they would ask for a full refund. For these Chinese businesses, perfection is do or die. It took several years before I had the time to really learn who was on the other side of the transaction.

The first time I imported for resale, I was looking to earn some extra cash. I had just finished self-publishing two Xbox indie games while working on a third 3D game, when Xbox privately announced they were ending their indie program, and wouldn't support self-publishing in the future. Being the opportunist I was, I wanted to try something new and somehow convinced my local college to let me set-up a table across from their bookstore and sell anything I wanted to.

With a primary demographic of students enrolled in technology, I imported and sold electronics for less than their bookstore including server cables, flash drives, and over 2,000 phone cables.

Although it was my first time importing products in bulk, I learned four valuable lessons:

First, I learned if I imported products for resale, I needed to immediately get a GST number and start collecting GST from my customers.

Second, DHL and FedEx could deliver anything I wanted from China to North America within just three business days.

Third, I discovered I was able to negotiate with suppliers for free DHL and FedEx shipping, as long as I bought $300 USD worth of products.

Fourth, if I promised these suppliers the possibility of a $10,000 order, I could get incredibly low pricing on a 'sample order' to verify quality.

By this time, I had my table setup at the college for several weeks. One morning I had several customers come up to my table and mention they were interested in buying flash drives. After searching on eBay, I found a five star supplier from Singapore and placed an order for 200 flash drives.

I believed I would not be scammed if I motivated my suppliers by telling them my next order would be ten times larger.

When the flash drives arrived, they worked like real flash drives. However, if anyone transferred files to them, they would instantly become corrupt and unusable. While I contacted eBay, and luckily was able to ship them back for a refund, I still learned a powerful lesson.

I wanted to make sure this never happened again. Through much research, I found a website called ChinaFlashMarket.com which shows the real cost of flash storage, which revealed my obvious mistake. I ordered flash drives for a lower price than the materials it would cost to make them. For the price I paid, there was no way they would have been able to manufacture these and deliver them with 3-day shipping, while still making a profit. Upon further research, I also found a program online called H2TESTw which verifies the real capacity of flash drives, and CrystalDisk-Mark, which confirms their real read/write speeds.

As time went on, I did find a quality supplier for flash drives, which helped me land a wholesale contract with the college itself.

As time went on, I finished selling electronics at the college. However, I still had a surplus of phone cables to sell. After seeing all this eCommerce hype, I thought it was time to give it a try. On eBay, my lowest cost competitor was selling these same phone cables for $0.99 with two-month shipping. Because I bought my phone cables in bulk, I was able to source them for $0.15 each; however, I still had to charge $1.80 in shipping, which was too expensive. However, I realized if I sold bulk packages of phone cables, I could combine shipping and sell them at a lower price than $0.99 in China!

Business started booming, and it quickly became time to rent a postage meter. Not only did it provide a 20% discount on shipping, but it also saved a lot of time, letting me weigh and stamp each package, then call Canada Post to pick them up, instead of having to drop off a shipment daily.

While everything seemed like it was going great, trouble struck. Overnight customers started to send photos of their phone cables cut in half. Apparently, Canada Post's sorting machines could only sort flat packages. They weren't able to handle irregular shaped cables within an envelope, and our cables were being shredded in their machines.

To ensure these cables could still securely travel through the mail, I purchased mini cardboard boxes for $0.20 each, which fit within Canada Post's oversized letter dimensions. Although costly, I never had another damaged package dispute again.

I continued researching new ways to expand, including drop shipping products from China directly to customers. What I found was most of our customers wouldn't wait longer than two weeks for their order. If they had to wait two months for shipping, the results were a nightmare.

Instead, by importing in bulk, not only was I able to offer more competitive pricing, but I was also able to test and clean products before re-shipping them, helping weed out as high as a 25% defect rate on some of our shipments.

Now that I had the proper systems in place, everything was running smoothly. I had over 98%+ positive reviews, my business continued to grow with 10+ orders per day, and I even had a dozen new product lines. However, without realizing it, I was being targeted, leading to the reason I was banned from eBay.

Apparently, it's common on eBay for scammers to target sellers who don't provide tracking numbers. These scammers would buy products for every member of their family. Then, after a month, they would open a dispute saying they never received their orders. PayPal would then instantly refund them for their orders due to no tracking information. With all the refunds occurring at once, eBay sent me an email saying they had permanently banned my account.

It was such a shame. However, I knew I could restart from scratch if I wanted to. If not eBay, then Amazon. However, while selling $10,000 per month did feel amazing, only 10% of that was profit, and it required working 80 hours per week to maintain it. Ecommerce was simply a penny profit game on the path to buying yourself a job.

Although I did later try Amazon FBA (Fulfillment by Amazon), which shipped products on my behalf, both of these market places were simply too competitive for generic products, unless I imported a 20-foot shipping container. While this would have saved me a whopping 50% on my products, it also requires an investment of about $30,000 to do so.

With that size order, I would have needed to fly to China to inspect the products before the container shipped. Three months later when the container would have arrived, there were no guarantees: that the demand for the products would still exist, whether someone else might also have had the great idea to order a container of the same products, if a price war might develop between similar sellers, and whether there would even be enough demand to sell an entire container of products.

However, I didn't give up or settle for less.

It was during this period that I became motivated to stop battling online for the lowest price, and instead start my first real business, importing products to sell at trade shows across Canada.

Not sure what a trade show is? Imagine travelling across the country with your closest friends and dozens of business owners, to events which have up to 1.2 million attendees, where everyone has a smile on their face while looking to buy anything that's even the slightest bit exciting.

This was a very important step in the right direction. It completely changed how I understood business, and it was profitable enough to hire a 12 member sales team.

I will talk about this and more in the next lesson.

★★★★★

Journey of a Travelling Salesman

I'm a fan of simple business models.

While many may see their simplicity and call them get-rich-quick-schemes, they still take hard work and time to achieve.

Most people overlook the fact that a business needs to be simple, and profitable enough to hire a team so we can one day replace ourselves.

After I finished my eCommerce business, even though there was still some potential, in the same way I decided to stop pursuing video game development even though there was still some potential, I decided the next step towards achieving my dreams was to continue importing products, but to sell them locally, instead of online.

When selling products online, I never had the opportunity to get to know my customers. I found it quickly became a race for the lowest price in a highly competitive environment, where all ethics were abandoned.

When selling products locally, I could take the time to really understand who my clients were and build amazing relationships with them. They were able to truly experience these products first-hand, and there was no competition, as I was the only one in the area who had these products.

While selling products online resulted in a battle for the lowest price, I could sell products locally for their full perceived value, allowing me to hire and help put food on the tables of 12 people.

Starting with only $1,000, left over from an income tax refund, I purchased my first product line of quadcopters and remote-controlled cars. Eventually, I would add other product lines: inflatable couches, skincare, graphical pillowcases, GPS trackers, and LED lights. By buying in bulk, I could order products at half their retail price, quickly doubling my money with each transaction.

By setting up a booth at a trade show, I was able to sell these products to thousands of people walking by. If a weekend booth cost me $600, I could easily sell $3500 worth of products. With a 50% product cost of $1,750, I would walk away with a $1,150 profit after just two and a half days of talking with people.

When looking for the ideal trade show to sell at, the four most important factors were:

1. The amount of people attending the event divided by the cost to attend.

While some events only cost $80 for over 1,000 attendees, others cost $80 for under 100 attendees or $800 for 1,000 attendees. Unless you have a niche product built for a specific audience at a specific event, it's simply a numbers game, and you don't want to waste your time, money, or motivation by attending events with barely any attendees.

2. Is the booth indoors or outdoors?

If the event has outdoor activities, odds are they will have an indoor exhibitor hall to shelter exhibitors from the rain. You, however, will want to beg the event coordinator to allow your booth to be outdoors as indoor exhibitor halls can have as low as 10% of the total event traffic.

While you will need a strong canopy, and stormy weather can quickly fatigue your staff, it's a risk you have to take, and plan for ahead of time. My highest sales days were outdoors, selling over $10,000 worth in a single day.

A well-structured 10' x 20' canopy will have no problems during stormy weather if it has the proper storm flaps, tied down to concrete blocks, and everything inside is standing on pallets. With a large enough canopy, you'll find customers regularly take shelter in your store during moments of heavy rain!!

With outdoor events, be prepared to pack up your booth every night, and setup every morning.

3. Get as close as you can to the entrance.

Attendees quickly become numb to all the signs and sounds after the first few booths. By half way through, odds are they've already spent all the money they're going to spend, or are tired of lengthy conversations with sales people, avoiding booths altogether.

4. If you can, always buy a corner booth.

For $100 more, you can significantly increase your traffic and have more room to display products. Line your products around the perimeter of your booth, customers want to touch and feel everything before they buy.

To save money on electricity, buy a portable battery. I bought a massive 40lb 1,000 watt pure-sine pack for $800. Instead of spending $100 for electricity at each event, I was able to power my entire booth, plus a TV, for a whole weekend.

Using the above tips, I was able to slowly grow year after year, causing both my profits and expenses to continually increase. Eventually, I was spending as much as $40,000 per month to hire

12 staff, selling half a dozen product lines, and exhibiting at events such as the Calgary Stampede and Edmonton K Days, which combined had over two million attendees.

Although everything looked simple on paper, trade shows were actually very expensive to sell at, with upfront costs requiring payment months in advance. This included rent for our booths, event passes, transportation costs, hotels, as well as inventory. After the trade show, we still needed to pay for our staff, EI, CPP, as well as debit terminal fees.

Regardless of our expectations, trade show sales were changing drastically year after year. Although the attendance averaged the same, the difference was whether people came to shop, or to simply look around. While our team pushed on, the majority of business owners around us would meet for coffee, and blame their low sales on natural disasters, an overly dry or wet season, recessions, unmotivated staff, pricing, etc. Personally, if I felt down, one of my favorite things to blame was the exchange rate.

When I first started importing in 2013, the Canadian and US dollar were both worth the same due to the 2008 US recession. However, as time went on, the US dollar slowly increased to its normal levels. Within three years of starting my business, from 2013 to 2016, Canada would see their dollar devalue by as much as 45%, meaning I would have to spend 45% more to import the same products!!

As many customers didn't realize this or care, they expected the same low price every year. After all, with automation everything should be getting cheaper, right? It was during this time Alibaba became well known. Everyone was asking us to price match with the US dollar cost of products from China, including tax!! What's worse is when we explained to them about how the exchange rate increased by 47%, how the government requires us to pay sales tax, how they'd be supporting local jobs, and how, if they ordered online from China, they would have to wait three months with no guarantee the product would even work when it arrived; they'd scoff and purposely stand beside us while purchasing the online products.

Within just a few years, it seemed like every customer switched to purchasing their products directly from China, instead of supporting local businesses. Combined with the low value of the dollar, I watched as many small businesses were unable to keep their staff employed, often closing their doors in the process. This brings me to my next point.

What was my favorite part about trade shows?

Where else could you go to immediately surround yourself with hundreds of local business owners? It was truly inspiring to see what one person could do, simply with an idea and a decent trade show display.

At each trade show I travelled to, I made sure to connect with as many business owners as possible. I wanted to understand everything about them, who they were, where they came from, their tips, their secrets, and their advice. After spending years listening to them, eerily, all their stories started to sound the same.

Many spent their lives traveling from trade show to trade show, staying for months at hotels with pools, being served fresh eggs and bacon every morning. How amazing the freedom felt when they could party the night away with their best friends every single night.

However, as time went on, they began to realize just how physically and mentally demanding trade shows were. Every week they had to book their next event, pay for hotels, purchase inventory, travel across provinces, build their display, perform high-pressure sales 12 hours/day for a week, pack up their display, update their accounting, and repeat the cycle, hopefully arriving on time for their next event.

As they grew older, they began to realize they no longer had the energy they used to and could not keep this up forever. They had to have a retirement plan in place, including passing the torch to the next generation.

Many tried to hire long-term staff, yet were unable to pay for a professional travelling sales team, especially after the cost of hotels, meals, and travelling. Instead, they were only able to afford to hire students during the summer.

> *I needed to find the answer, not only for my own business, but also for all those walking a similar path. I needed to break the cycle.*

While these students quickly learned how to sell, as always, talented staff know what they're worth and demand to be compensated accordingly. Also, after these students spent all summer being mentored, they would leave to open their own competing trade show businesses the following year. Unfortunately, they were only exposed to the basics, not realizing just how little profit there actually was, all the work that needed to be done behind the scenes, and how hard it would be for them to find talented staff themselves. In the end, they bought themselves a job, repeating the cycle.

After years of high turnover, eventually it came time for these business owners to pass the torch down to their children. However, as these children watched their parents become trapped by their own businesses, they became afraid of ever owning a business themselves.

Finally, when these business owners grew too old to keep up with all the physical work trade shows require, they had no choice but to close their business. Many were without a decent pension, and were never truly able to retire in the way they'd imagined. This was an unfortunate ending for someone who spent their entire life working harder than most, believing one day they might achieve the life they'd always dreamt about.

Although I was passionate about the trade show industry, I knew something was missing. I knew something separated mom and pop businesses from those with a salaried team, a board of directors, plus shareholders. I needed to find the answer, not only for my own business, but also for all those walking a similar path. I needed to break the cycle.

> *All we need to remember is,*
> *we can never allow our failures to be in vain.*

Although I didn't know what the answer was, I knew I wouldn't find it if I stayed on the same path. I had to shut down my business, liquidate everything, and focus my energy on something new. This is the point at which I decided to once again start over from scratch.

Not surprisingly, most business owners are afraid of starting all over again, even if their current business is losing money. The thought of closing their doors, being branded a failure, losing all the clients they spent years working to build relationships with, can all seem pretty scary. However, if your business simply isn't sustainable long term, you're only hurting yourself by not restarting, each time returning stronger than before.

Never be afraid to start over, even if it means switching to a completely different industry. While it may seem like you have nothing right now, you were born with everything you need to succeed. While most people will continue their entire lives pretending everything will work out, instead, take everything you've learned, the work ethic you've developed, all the contacts you've gained, and turn it into a successful business.

While you will probably sink into the deepest moments of doubt you will ever face, know that we can only see our successes after they've happened.

Take a moment to write down all the milestones which led to who you are today. Every time I feel unmotivated, I work on this list. While life feels like a series of constant failures, it's incredible to see how my achievements seem to double every year. I've grown from someone who has made two Xbox indie video games, to a thriving eCommerce business, to a trade show business with half a dozen product lines and sales people.

All we need to remember is, we can never allow our failures to be in vain.

Now, the next step in our journey awaits.

Regardless of what my next business would be, I knew it had to be profitable enough to afford a properly trained team, especially because those who are talented know what they're worth.

To afford fully trained professionals, not only would I need to pay for their salaries, bonuses, travelling costs, equipment, benefits, employment insurance, and pension plans, but I also would have to make sure that we could grow the company as a whole, so they could eventually manage their own departments.

To afford these high salaries, I realized most successful product-based businesses need their sales staff to sell an average of $240 per hour. That's over $500,000 per year, per salesperson!!

Although it's a lot, it's needed to pay for non-sales staff to fulfill the orders, marketing, accounting, IT departments, upper management, the office space, utilities, equipment, supplies, with leftovers for investments, growth, and finally shareholder dividends.

This is why it's so important to have the right systems in place, to maximize the sales per hour our sales team are able to make. If our sales team ended up spending half of their day simply preparing, they would need to double their hourly sales just to keep up!

Researching further into how large companies consistently perform on this level, I finally made a discovery that answered all of my questions. It took five years of trial and error, but I learned the secret about what separated mom and pop businesses from large scalable businesses.

That is, large scale businesses with a salaried team and a board of directors, whose owners were able to transition to the life of a board member.

Yet, nearly all B2B businesses are run by a board of directors and managed by high salaried professionals. Coincidence?

The answer lies in the difference between B2C (business to customer) and B2B (business to business). This means businesses which focus on selling directly to customers versus businesses which in some way focus on working with, and selling directly, to other businesses.

I, and many others, spent our lives focusing on selling directly to end customers. We knew what we wanted and tried to sell those products and services to people who had similar interests.

However, my perception changed when I realized one thing nearly all B2C business owners have in common; they bought themselves a job, requiring themselves to work forever to make ends meet.

Yet, nearly all B2B businesses are run by a board of directors and managed by high salaried professionals. Coincidence?

But wait. What about the large B2C businesses that we see every day?

Most people don't realize that almost all B2C businesses, which look successful, either have some form of B2B income, or franchise out the B2C part of their business so they only need to operate B2B with their new franchise owners.

This helps the franchisors save a lot of time and energy by removing the focus on the end customer. Instead, at a minimum, all they need to provide their franchisees are the tools needed to run their own operations, fulfill the franchisees' wholesale orders, and collect royalties on overall sales.

With an automated system, the franchisor takes in all wholesale orders and royalty payments with minimal work. By maximizing their sales per staff hour worked, franchisors can afford to pay their office staff more in a year than most B2C franchisees earn themselves.

After seeing how powerful B2B businesses were, I knew I needed to create my own. It wasn't difficult deciding what I wanted to sell either. My passion has always been about helping to create more jobs, what better way to accomplish this than by helping businesses save time, money, and energy?

To assist local businesses, I decided to try a new business model, sourcing products local companies were already buying, in hopes of saving them money.

During the fidget spinner craze of 2017, I had dozens of businesses across western Canada requesting them. Simply by emailing them a pdf price sheet and a PayPal invoice, I was now wholesaling as much as $20,000 per week entirely in pre-orders. Once a client placed a wholesale order, I would then contact our supplier in China, have them manufacture fidget spinners, ship them over the weekend, test them here in Canada, and still deliver the order to the client within 10 business days from when they first placed their order.

Using the above math, it was simple to see if I expanded into just a few more product lines for stability, and received just seven to eight orders per week, I could personally sell $1,560,000/year. Not too shabby!

However, owning a wholesale company didn't really excite me.

Don't you find it ironic, after spending years searching for the perfect business, I finally arrived at a point where I may have been able to build a successful business, then stopped simply to say, "It doesn't really excite me"?

At the end of the day, my business depended on selling products to clients. The more I sold, the better my business would be.

While I may have saved my clients money on products they were already buying, many of them were still barely able to keep their doors open, having less and less repeat customers each day. Each passing day was one day closer to being unable to pay their bills and inevitably closing their business.

While the wholesale company may have been a sales person's dream, I wanted a business to truly leave a legacy and help local businesses succeed.

Instead of solely focusing on products, I needed to focus and specialize. I spent so many years solving problems within my own business, why couldn't that information be useful in helping other businesses succeed?

One of the largest problems was that local businesses rarely know how to attract new customers. It's very difficult to get word of mouth out about your business, especially if your branding looks slapped together or hasn't been updated in over a decade.

This is especially true at trade shows, where many booths were simply a wooden table covered with a dollar store thin green plastic table cover. Then they would wonder why they weren't getting any sales.

Within my own booth, I realized 80% of our perceived value was through our display and product packaging alone.

Understanding this early on has helped me build a solid network of custom display and packaging contacts. I had already sold several custom displays to business owners who were envious of my display.

With my knowledge of importation, motivation to help businesses succeed, understanding of a client's mindset, and connections with professional branding suppliers, I decided to take the next leap and start NORTHERN EXHIBITS – A Physical Branding Agency.

With a diverse industry and much to learn, the only way to specialize in anything is to simply take your time.

I joined associations, found mentors, took courses, learned graphic design, and more importantly, I gained connections.

As the physical branding industry is diverse, it's impossible to know how to do everything. Anyone who thinks or says they do is naive. However, with a strong list of contacts, you can build a powerful business from referring clients alone. Then, when you hire someone to do a job you don't know how to do, learn from those you hire. You will retain that knowledge for the rest of your life.

Several years later, project after project, helping business after business, I am proud to be where I am, helping many local business owners along the way.

In the end, I can tell you switching to B2B was one of the best decisions I ever made.

So, where are we now?

NORTHERN EXHIBITS – A Physical Branding Agency, works together with over 35,000 North American businesses, helping clients maximize their profitability, better connect with their customers, and achieve overall success in today's volatile world.

Physical branding is much more than simply branding products. We focus on creating a cohesive brand image across all aspects of your business, tying in your organizations values and beliefs, while increasing your overall perceived value.

Extending across all industries, physical branding can go as far as turning concepts into reality, as we work with you to identify the best method and materials needed to bring your project to life.

★★★★★

Instinctual by Design

I really want you to succeed in both life and business.

As we work to become the best version of ourselves, often we reach our own limits and wonder what is wrong with us. Everyone else seems to be doing fine. Why should we be any different?

The reality is, we're all very different, and need to take very different approaches to find out what works for us.

As you can see, every author in this book has followed a very different path to get to where they are today. While some structured themselves by following proven concepts, others like myself spent years of trial and error trying to find out what does and doesn't work, with the hope of creating something new. No advice will work 100% for you, but take time to explore each path and see what does.

Before you begin your entrepreneurial journey, I want to make sure you're prepared for the road ahead. While it's easy to write about all the dangers around you, the greatest danger lies within you.

We need to understand how our bodies work, what makes us do the things we do, crave the things we crave. We also need to develop our mindset and program our instincts. Without understanding who we really are, we have no control over our own actions, letting history repeat itself and our failures become pointless. It's easy to blame external factors. In reality, we've had the power to create change all along.

Self-Awareness

The human mind is simpler than most people think.

When you feel like you need something, your brain searches for the best way to achieve it, using the least amount of energy. This is called "following the path of least resistance."

Before you make a decision, your brain has already calculated what it wants to do. While you can veto the decision at any time, when we're tired or fatigued we let our instincts guide us.

However, how does our brain decide which actions provide the best results? And, how can we hijack that process to control our basic instincts?

Let's take this one-step at a time.

Back when you were a child, it took you a long time to solve a math problem. Now, you probably can solve 10 x 10 without using your fingers. Each time you solve a problem, your brain records the path it took and prioritizes it for next time. As your brain builds more efficient pathways, you're able to solve more complex problems in a fraction of the time.

Remember when you could divide numbers with decimals? You might still remember the concept, but I bet it will take you several minutes to solve something which used to take you seconds. Although we're constantly building and prioritizing new pathways, we eventually forget paths that aren't used as often. This means the best way to remember a skill is to practice it.

Our instincts also heavily rely on these pathways. When we neglect our needs, such as skipping lunch so we can work longer, our instincts start to crave the easiest method towards fulfilling those needs. As our cravings intensify, to the point where we cannot ignore them any longer, we finally succumb to our hunger and resort to eating a bag full of greasy, deep fried potato chips or whatever else we have handy.

When we're faced with a new decision, we must think. Thinking requires energy, which wears us down. To save energy, once we make a decision, our brain saves it and prioritizes it as the best way to solve the problem, changing our instincts, our cravings, even who we are in the process.

> *While we feel like we have self-control, it's the habits we've created through repetition which shape the way we work, feel, and live.*

Although we can rationalize eating unhealthy foods by saying "just this one time", if we continue to choose potato chips when we're hungry, our brain prioritizes potato chips as the best solution to hunger, to the point that we no longer have to decide whether we want to eat chips. The answer is always yes.

While we feel like we have self-control, it's the habits we've created through repetition which shape the way we work, feel, and live. If we let our habits get the best of us, they can quickly become addictions. While we might not realize we're addicted, when our potato chips run out, we can quickly become irritable as we search for something else to fill the void.

Submitting to our addictions make us weak, needy, insecure, and demanding. It takes work and real effort to consistently make different choices and break bad habits.

The good news is, as simple as it is to program yourself with unhealthy habits, you can also re-program yourself with better, healthier habits. By understanding what your body is actually asking for when it craves something, and providing your body with a healthier solution to the problem, your brain will slowly prioritize the newer, healthier habits. It's why you hear people say, after being on a diet for several weeks, they've finally started to crave healthier foods and have much more energy.

Although I'm using food as an example, this principle applies to all decisions one makes, such as constantly allowing yourself to become distracted by your phone, your co-workers, or even social media. If this happens repeatedly, your brain will prioritize these, making you feel the need to resolve all the above before you're able to begin working on your daily to-do list. By focusing on prioritizing your work above all else during the time you've set aside for work, you can accomplish twice as much, preventing yourself from having too many things occupy your brain at once, creating decision fatigue.

Re-programming your mind is one of the easiest ways to change your life, as you learn to control your habits. This is why so many top entrepreneurs love the concept of daily affirmations. Every morning they wake up, look in the mirror, and chant to themselves to "be the change they want to see in the world." You can change who you are through words alone.

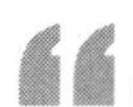

Sometimes we don't need to change. We just need to let ourselves know that being us is all we need to be.

If you're unsure what your daily affirmations should be, simply write down your vision of the world you want to create. Write down who it is you're fighting for, and why you would risk everything to win. Write down why your vision makes you an unstoppable force, and why you keep coming back year after year, stronger than before. Write down your plan to win, and why no one can tell you otherwise. Finally, write down why you love you, for you.

When we feel pressured to be more than we feel capable of, it's okay to tell ourselves we did our best. We are the best version of ourselves we could possibly be, given our circumstances. We're not like anyone else. We are who we are and we're proud of how far we've come.

Sometimes we don't need to change. We just need to let ourselves know that being us is all we need to be.

Once you've written it all down, re-read it, and update it every morning. You'll achieve much more than you ever imagined.

> *"your brain can only make so many decisions each day, based on how well you're sleeping, eating, and exercising"*

Self-awareness is one of the most important keys to success, and is what separates entrepreneurs from the most well-known business owners today. They've become successful because they have spent years studying how they themselves work, as well as those in the world around them.

If you understand the psychology behind why people do the things they do, then you begin to understand your clients, know what problems they may have, even before they do, and can adapt your business to more adequately address their needs. For example, grocery stores with the right systems in place have been able to examine their shopper's purchasing habits and accurately market baby products to women who were not even aware they were pregnant yet!

Mental Fatigue

The blessing of being an entrepreneur is there's always problems waiting to be solved and there's always something waiting to be done. To be self-aware is to understand your body's needs and to know when it's time to take a break. When you take a break, you refresh and recharge.

Whether you know it or not, your brain can only make so many decisions each day, based on how well you're sleeping, eating, and exercising. Each decision taxes your brain, including what you plan on wearing for the day, what time to eat, and even whether you should respond to that text message you just received. Each decision accumulates, exhausting most people within six hours of continuous work.

It's why many famous billionaires live a very simplistic day-to-day lifestyle, almost always choosing the same style clothes, ordering the same food and following the same routines.

They understand, if they can delegate 20 smaller decisions so they only need to focus on the one final decision, now they can solve 20 final decisions using a similar amount of energy. Not only does it give them a 20x performance/productivity increase each day, but it also helps them maintain the composure they need to lead their team toward a vision, instead of looking like an overworked, stressed-out ball of tension.

While delegating is important, we can also increase the amount of productive decisions we make each day, by simply creating a peaceful distraction-free work environment. This is an area where we disconnect ourselves from our personal lives, social media, email, and cellphone.

By having separate emails, phone numbers, and social media accounts for work, we can limit our distractions while working, but also disconnect our minds from work once we're outside of the office. There's no point in making complex decisions when we're unable to take the time to do proper research, or act, once we've come up with a conclusion.

Our brains can only make so many decisions before they become fatigued, so don't be afraid to take a mid-day nap. You'll find they recharge you, giving much needed time to reflect. It's said only in moments of pure boredom do we have thoughts of pure genius.

Forgetfulness

We all forget. By the time you're done reading this book, you'll probably forget nearly everything you have read. Because of this, many top business owners say they re-read their favorite books at least three times. Initially to under-stand what the book's about, the second time to grasp underlying concepts, and a third time to memorize the content so they can recite and teach it by memory.

We all forget and it's easy to let the knowledge from any book go to waste. Instead, when you read a book for the first time, highlight key concepts you feel would be valuable to memorize or use for personal improvement.

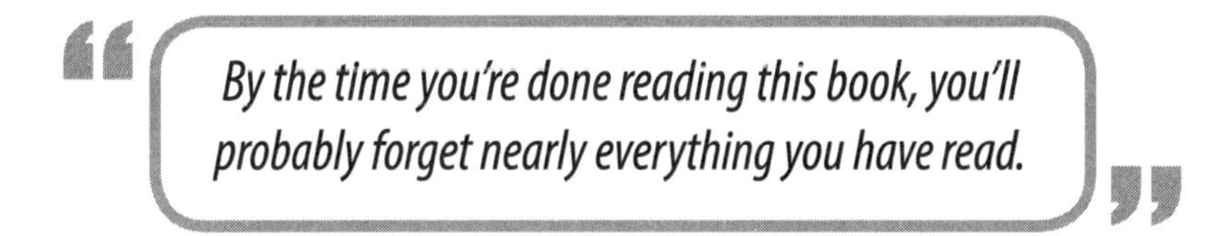

The second time you read the book, grab a notepad and write down the highlighted sections you feel still have value or you need to improve on. Make sure to write down the page number next to them.

The third reading of a book would indicates you believe the book has value, and you've probably started to see results in your own life. Take everything you've written down in your notebook and prioritize which concepts you believe are the most powerful. Write them on the front of a cue card. On the back of the cue card, write down which concepts you still need to work on.

Once every 3-6 months, go through your box of cue cards and continue to study each of the concepts. Those are the concepts that will make you rich, and are valuable to others just like yourself.

Because we all forget, these cue cards are going become your golden treasure chest of knowledge. They will remind you of everything important, and guide you on your path to success. Take care of them and they will take care of you.

Abstract Metrics

When planning how you'll reach a goal, such as saving up enough money to buy a van, it's easy to come up with a simple solution with measurable results, for example, telling your sales team they need to sell $10,000 each week until you can afford a car from the profits. This is known as concrete metrics.

The problem with concrete metrics is they assume every problem is exactly the same. It means the "three strikes and you're out" rule applies to every person in every circumstance. Given an expectation in which the sales team needs to sell $10,000 per week, is often interpreted by staff as, "we don't have to worry about profits, growth, or long-term investments. All we need to focus on is sales."

This seemingly harmless method of goal setting allows both staff and management to develop a narrow focus, create a less productive environment, hinder performance, bringing results drastically short of where they could be, if only goals were set with abstract metrics in mind.

Instead of concrete metrics, which puts the focus on a single path towards success, abstract metrics directs the focus to overall success.

Instead of focusing on the fact we need to sell $10,000 per week so we can eventually buy a car, abstract metrics would shift the goal from the narrow focus of sales, to the final objective of obtaining the car itself. This allows staff better use of their time. Especially if John knows a guy selling a car for cheap, Joe has a great relationship with a shop owner if any repairs are needed, and

Jim is an expert when it comes to negotiating vehicle prices, all while realizing we could trade our services for the van, thus saving us thousands of dollars in up-front capital.

Even if increasing sales was the only option, as a business owner it's important to teach staff the difference between sales and profit, focusing on increasing profit whenever there's an opportunity.

By changing how your team's success is measured, as close as possible to the final outcome we want to achieve, we allow staff to come up with their own solutions to the problem, saving money on expenses they may have otherwise spent, finding ways to cut costs and increase profit where possible, and work with us towards achieving a common goal.

Society

Society and media assure us, if we work hard enough, we can afford anything we want. Mansions, sports cars, travelling the world, or simply a nice quiet farm in the country.

They say all these things give us status, and that somehow automatically translates to include friends, passion, excitement, adventure, freedom, and most importantly, our independence.

These advertisements however, are dangerous. They can convince an entire generation to work their entire lives with the hope of one day affording their dreams. They are being sold unrealistic expectations of what life can offer them, but are never able to achieve it, many people give up along the way feeling worthless, while those few who do achieve their dreams realize they're missing an important part of their life.

You see, achieving financial freedom is one of the loneliest feelings in the world. Your business friends are always working, focused on their next big project and their own priorities, while your non-business friends feel jealous and inferior, having to work multiple jobs over the next 30 years of their lives, earning just enough to provide for their families.

You realize this when everyone around you is complaining about work and their bosses. They ask you how your day was, then they remember you don't have the same problems they do. You're different. Every day is a vacation for you, while your friends are constantly struggling. You say to yourself, "Well they could start their own businesses, and I can help!!" But they simply don't want to. They're not business people, and they don't want to be.

It becomes tough because you have everything you want, yet feel disconnected from everyone, lacking relationships with real people who truly know who you are, and are there for you. Imagine making friends all over the world, yet going home to none.

"*money is just a tool, and there will always be someone happier than us who earns far less than we do.*"

While you've made it, everyone around you hasn't. They still need to work. They still come home exhausted after work every day, still need to take care of chores and spend time with their family, only to start over the next day to the sound of their 5 a.m. alarm. Much like you used to do.

Although money can help us buy our freedom, it's important to know money is just a tool, and there will always be someone happier than us who earns far less than we do.

While the meaning of life is an age-old question, it has always been a red herring. The meaning of life isn't distilled into a single meaning at all, but it is up to us to create meaning.

The secret to happiness isn't to buy into status, but rather to focus on building up those around us, so they too may achieve success, creating a strong community in the process. It's only when others succeed that we succeed, guiding us towards a happier life.

Community

It has been incredible how much my life has changed, simply by believing "the only way I will ever be successful is if I make sure those who are around me become successful first".

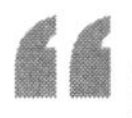

the only way I will ever be successful is if I make sure those who are around me become successful first".

The result of helping other entrepreneurs was that they chose to reciprocate, we also began to form a community, working together to cross promote each other's businesses, creating new connections that I never dreamed of having access to. In fact, almost everyone I know today was at some point referred to me by those whom I could help.

Leadership

When you are a leader in the community, it's easy to take everyone's struggles upon yourself. If a single person fails, you feel like you failed too.

A real leader isn't remembered because they won or lost a war, but how they led their followers through the hardships involved.

Too many people are afraid of being leaders because they feel they don't know enough, therefore they are afraid of leading their followers to failure. However, I encourage you to research the Dunning–Kruger effect, which states: dumb people think they're smart, and smart people think they're dumb.

> *A real leader isn't remembered because they won or lost a war, but how they led their followers through the hardships involved.*

Because of this, remember there's always someone dumber and less ethical than you, who's more confident in their ability to lead your followers, sell to your clients, and take action where you're not, giving a bad name to your industry in the process.

If you think you're dumb, realize it only takes one full day of education to be more well-informed about a subject than 99% of the world's population.

Clients can smell the difference between someone who's genuine, versus simply hunting for a sale. As someone who's genuine, you'll be surprised how much support your clients will give you, if you treat them like actual human beings.

Five Steps to Making a Sale

A new customer walks up to your business. Based on first impressions alone, how much money would they feel comfortable spending based on your brand?

One of the most overlooked aspects of any business is its appearance, from a hole-in-the-wall noodle shop serving discount $2.50 rice dishes, to a full-scale Michelin-Star restaurant serving $40 risottos, featuring premium flavors from around the world. Before ever stepping inside, potential customers judge the value of these restaurants, only buying from those which they feel align with their values and taste.

While premium customers exist, and are willing to spend extra for quality service, surprisingly, most business owners focus on budget-minded customers simply looking for the lowest priced services, who will switch suppliers the second they find a better deal.

> *The reality is, when you advertise your services for the lowest dollar, you're telling everyone how little you think you're worth.*

Regardless of this, many budget shops believe the secret to success is advertising their services at the lowest price possible, with the belief that they can slowly increase their prices later. Believe me, I've been there. The reality is, when you advertise your services for the lowest dollar, you're telling everyone how little you think you're worth.

After being left with a non-existent profit, you won't be able to afford reliable staff, forcing yourself to work harder than is healthy, while preventing yourself from focusing on properly expanding your business. Also, if customers do have any issues, you probably won't have the money to fix their problems, thus causing much undue stress.

I'm not saying you should charge your customers excessive amounts, but instead write down all the value you offer and research how much successful companies in your area are charging, for similar levels of value. By successful, I mean consider companies which have been around for longer than a decade, with owners who were able to replace themselves with a self-sustaining team.

Perhaps the prices you arrive at will be higher than you're comfortable with. Instead of lowering your prices, your job is to find ways to provide your customers with real value, combined with a sincere effort to build real relationships over several years, while finding ways you can offer both the best solution for their needs, through the best experience possible. Only then will it become extremely difficult for any competitor to prove themselves superior. Actions always speak louder than words.

While deciding how we can develop a superior brand, the best offering, with proper rates so we can hire a talented team, we need to ask ourselves, how much do we need to sell per year to achieve a sustainable business?

Seriously. Write down what you expect to sell this year, how much your anticipated expenses are after hiring your ideal team, and how much profit you'll be left with at the end of the year. Take an hour and map it all out.

Most new business owners will see this estimated profit, become very motivated, and will push themselves to do whatever it takes to achieve it. That is, until sales are lower than expected, new costs appear, your best staff ask for higher pay or threaten to leave, you need capital for growth, and most importantly, you forgot you and your team can't achieve your best every day.

Instead of focusing on a profit like $100,000 per year, imagine what it would take to make double the profit. $200,000. Seriously, draw it out. If your average order was the same size, and you had to help ten times the customers in the same amount of time, would your business be structured the same way it is now? How big would your team need to be? What technologies would you use to automate time-consuming tasks? Can you afford to have the proper management in place? Does your ideal team even exist given the salary you're offering? Although drastic, if you don't plan for growth, it's unlikely you'll even achieve your original goal.

You see, people always fall short of their own goals. In order to be an Olympic gold medalist, you need to raise the bar far higher than anyone else. It's no longer a competition with anyone but yourself. You need to set an impossible goal and become devastated if you fall short. A true Olympian falling short of their own goal is still good enough for gold.

By having a $200,000 mindset, you may have a terrible sales year and only accumulate a $100,000 profit, but because of this you will have achieved your original goal. If you had only planned for a $100,000 profit, you might have had an equally terrible sales year, only achieving a $50,000 profit.

Once you plan it out, a $200,000 profit per year doesn't seem too difficult with the right service, the right team, and the right vision.

However, why would we ever need such a high profit anyway?

Shocking to most, successful businesses typically need to spend over $500,000 per year to afford a team of reliable, professional staff, capable of replacing you, so you have the option of enjoying an early retirement whenever you please.

Given your profit margins, if you need to sell $1,000,000 per year to afford that, it means business owners with a successful mindset need at least a $2,000,000/year mentality.

If this sounds difficult, you may need to automate your existing business, switch your business model, or move to a more suitable location.

With the right product or service, once you have the proper systems in place, all that's left to do is sell.

But how does one sell?

Let's start with the fundamentals. These five steps are for those who want to learn the tactics I've learned throughout my time in sales.

#1: Sell the Dream

Luxurious brands appear to have customers throwing fists full of cash their way. Yet, what is it that makes luxurious brands luxurious? After all, many of these brands sell the same products as everyone else, plus a few minor adjustments and a private label.

Whether it's that sleek minimalist design, the story behind the brand, an online community, or their fast and friendly customer support, luxurious brands wrap their products in a unique service you just can't find anywhere else.

When a luxurious brand solves a problem, they really go out of their way to solve it through providing the best experience possible.

A luxurious brand encompasses more than a simple focus on high status. Potential customers will walk away if they feel like you're trying to manipulate them to buy through sales tactics, like appealing to a desire for status or popularity. Instead, your customers are searching for something deeper, a product or service they feel will lead to a happier overall life. If you can connect to your customers, find out their needs, and talk about how your products or services can provide them with a happier life, they'll not only buy, but they'll refer you to everyone they know! Why wouldn't they want to help their friends and family become happier too?

You're probably thinking, how you can sell the concept of happiness? After selling various products and services, it's easy to realize it doesn't matter what you sell. People will generally buy anything they feel emotionally attached to, with trending products having the strongest emotional attachments. Simply put, if you can emotionally attach your demographic to your products and they're able to find the cash for it, you've made a sale. A great advertising campaign can help sell just about anything, with people coming back for more.

One of the best examples of this is a simple product called the pet rock. A rock is a rock. The secret isn't to sell based on specifications, but based on outcomes.

Specifications: Here is a blue and glossy rock.

Outcomes: This pet rock will provide your children with weeks of fun and enjoyment while they learn the responsibilities they need for their first real pet.

However, beyond simply selling outcomes, luxurious brands also create a highly emotional story around their products.

People naturally use empathy to understand how others feel and a powerful story with relatable characters or personified objects will naturally make viewers feel those same powerful emotions themselves, often connecting those powerful emotions to the very brands you want them to become addicted to.

While many people think they can resist subliminal messaging, our brains prioritize the most frequent thoughts. If we continue to think about an advertisement after we've seen it, we're much more likely to remember the brand once were ready to shop the market.

Shock messages also work very well, pushing the boundaries of what's acceptable, and it helps spread your message. However, it doesn't work for all demographics. If people feel negatively about your message, it can be a quick way to lose your following.

When it comes to selling via emotions, nearly everyone dreams of a world where their problems no longer exist, they imagine a world where they've found the freedom or independence they've truly desired.

However, simply advertising an ideal world isn't enough. Most people can't relate to it because they haven't yet reached it. Instead, it's much more effective to advertise through a success story.

Imagine you're watching an advertisement featuring an individual who is struggling with their business. Through failure after failure they cannot seem to do anything right. Then, someday, by some luck, they muster the courage to reach out for help and it's your brand which comes flying to the rescue. Not only do you solve their problems through teamwork, thus turning their life around, but they also decide to thank you by paying it forward. They start giving back to the community. Instead of failing, they start succeeding. As a result of building new relationships, they are now part of something much greater than themselves. Everyone around them is happy, and together they achieve their own version of success.

Although this sounds cliché, it works, and million-dollar companies are constantly profiting from it.

Finally, when 'selling the dream', be creative. You might not believe your product is capable of changing the world, but remember, diamond engagement rings have only existed since the 1930s. Now it's a billion dollar industry and a way of life for most of the world.

Like diamond engagement rings, everything we know now was at one point sold to us by others, or even sold to us by ourselves. The way our brain works is, if we can't disprove it, it becomes a possibility. Equally, if our brain can't disprove an advertised product will give us happiness, then we naturally believe there's a possibility it could do so.

#2: Make Them Crave It

After selling the dream and connecting with your clients emotionally, you need your clients to crave what you're selling. Everyone has basic instincts, wants, and needs. As hardships occur, people tend to neglect very important parts of their lives, creating stress and leaving room for fantasies to grow. This includes fantasizing about freedom, their next adventure, meeting new people, or simply living a happier life.

There are many ways to make people crave what you have. One is to focus on the six senses: taste, sight, touch, smell, sound, and gravity.

Right now, imagine that you and a group of friends decide to jump off a plane flying at 12,000 feet. As you're quickly falling towards the ground with the rush of wind against your face, you smell the fresh cold air and can even taste it as you breathe. Everyone around you is laughing while having the time of their lives. Several are even taking selfies. You're almost touching the ground now. You quickly pull your parachute, jerking you into an upright position. As you hit the ground you think to yourself, although your first fall was frightening, it was a rush unlike anything else.

You can also make people crave what you have by targeting their biggest problems. Whether that's displaying hot, greasy food to hungry people walking through a mall, or finding out what difficulties businesses are facing and showing them how your solution perfectly solves every one of their problems.

When advertising to clients, it's important to understand the majority are exhausted and simply don't have the time for what you're selling. The only way to sell to these clients is by making your product 'the path of least resistance'. It's only after you position your solution as the easiest one to solve their problems that they'll genuinely become interested, and willing to use what little energy they have remaining to hear you out. Once they crave your product, they've already sold themselves and are now simply looking for reasons not to buy. At this point, the less you talk, the more sales you'll close.

#3: Building Trust

A lack of trust is the main reason clients decide not to buy. Whether it's because they don't trust the industry, your brand, your products, or how you look, it's important to remove any sense of pride you may feel and focus on staying genuine. Connect with them on a personal level, listen to their needs, show them you truly care, and prove to them you're worthy of their business.

Clients look at many factors when they're making a purchase. They care about whether your branding and sales team are professional, if the value exceeds the cost, what after sales support looks like, where the products are made, and whether you can solve their problems. Surprisingly, many sales people say the only reason a client agreed to work with them on a large project, was because they were the only one who answered their phone at 5 a.m. It's the small things that build trust, especially if you're always there when your client needs you.

When building a sales team, it's very easy to hire someone who looks professional, only to have them turn into a money-motivated shark. Often highly charismatic, sharks see clients as a numbers game and will fake their way through the sale using any means necessary. They're easily spotted through their aggressive tactics or overtly charismatic demeanor.

Sharks quickly create a negative reputation for your business, losing the trust of your clients along the way. After all, your clients would rather spend money working with someone who takes the time to build a real relationship.

As a business owner, it's also important to know high pressure deadlines can quickly make sharks out of good employees. You need to make sure reasonable goals are stated, with frequent deadlines to avoid any last minute tensions. If you feel you have to optimize your business to the point your sales people turn into sharks, your business model has larger problems than just profit, especially once you start losing all of your clients.

If you do identify sales staff who become desperate, find ways to help them before they start to use aggressive sales tactics to close sales. Although a client may be happy with you now, all it takes is one bad experience for them to silently switch to a competitor. By building a strong relationship your clients today, you'll prove that your brand is worthy of their loyalty.

#4: Give So Much Value, They Feel Guilty Not Buying

This one is simple. People love to support and see the success of businesses who go out of their way to help others. Whether it's a free app which saves time and effort, a blog with the latest tips and tricks, an industry-networking event for like-minded people, or even a storefront, which hosts free workshops, clients appreciate the extra effort.

If people frequently receive things of value from you for free, and believe that you're doing it genuinely to help others, they'll feel more inclined to buy something from you, especially if you send them a personal offer which feels too good to be true.

#5: Give an offer they can't refuse.

By now, your clients should know how all the products and services in your offer work, as well have a decent idea of how much it costs at full retail pricing. All you need to close the sale is that one final push. An offer they simply cannot refuse.

While you may want to give discounts, clients have no problem negotiating, asking for further discounts. Instead, if you offer smaller add-on items for free, instead of discounting a larger item, your final sale price will typically be higher, and you can avoid long negotiations as clients don't want to look bad asking for additional free add-ons.

However, free add-ons can still eat away at your profits. Instead, we'll look at a couple of methods which will cost you next to nothing.

The first method is to give them the most expensive gift available: knowledge.

Anyone can do physical labor for minimum wage. Its knowledge and experience which separates executives from the work force. The key is to try and create a collection of knowledge considered of high value to your clients. Don't write down every thought you have, but only those concepts your clients would pay their staff to figure out, such as how they can build a physical brand, new ways they can better reach their clients, creating scalable systems to help run their business more efficiently, and how they can improve sales to earn higher profits.

Not sure if you know something which could upgrade their business? If your business focuses on solving a client's problem, there's a good chance their problem was created due to a lack of education in that area. By creating and packaging quality digital educational content such as videos, guides, how-to's, and audiobooks, you'll be able to educate your clients so they're better equipped to handle these problems in the future.

Not only will your clients be more informed, but it's an opportunity to show them you're an expert at what you do.

Here are some other items that businesses bundle for free: extended warranties, one-on-one training, onsite set-up, public promotion of their client's business, unlimited future upgrades, or my favorite, barter.

As my business revolves around Physical Branding, if a sandwich shop was looking for quotes on a new sign or wanted someone to supply them with $1,000 worth of printed products, I could offer them a barter deal where they only pay us $500 in cash and the remaining $500 in gift certificates.

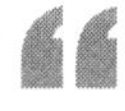

Top companies should push referrals to make up at least 80% of their client base

Assuming the cost of their sandwich ingredients are fairly low, it's likely they're only spending $200 in ingredients per $500 worth of sales. As they're paying $500 in cash and their gift cards are only costing them $200 worth of ingredients, they will feel like they're only spending $700 for $1,000 worth of products. When comparing quotes, I will always win, as $700 cost is lower than anything anyone else will bid.

To seal the deal, I would also promise the sandwich shop I'd give away the $500 in gift certificates to my clients as gifts, potentially bringing the sandwich shop new long-term clients they didn't have before. If the clients like the sandwich shop, it could lead to potential catering orders in the future. This strategy alone is the secret to how I win clients from even my most cutthroat competitors.

I've sold physical branding in exchange for legal services, web development, landscaping, vehicle repairs, paintball, airsoft, go karts, catering, wine, pitas, perogies, honey, baking, and much more.

Finally, after you make the sale, ask for referrals. Incentivize it by sharing a portion of the profits one way or another. Top companies should push referrals to make up at least 80% of their client base. As long as you can make your clients happy, they will be more than pleased to share you with their network.

I hope you enjoyed these five steps. While short, they're easy to apply wherever you are, whether at a board meeting, a mall kiosk, or a televised sales pitch. Right now, you know everything you need to know. It's time to go execute, live a life of constant learning, and pay it forward by sharing your knowledge with the world.

While it may be tempting to gloss over certain sections of this book, they wouldn't be in here unless they had an important place in creating who we are today, taking many years to discover. Please, spend at least one weekend reading this book thoroughly. It may result in you living the best years of your life.

We're also human, like you. Get in touch. Ask for advice. Chat about business. Don't let where you are right now get in the way of where you can be. If we didn't believe in you, we wouldn't have taken the time to write this book for you.

★★★★★

Why I Contributed to this Book

We have only two choices in life. We can either try to fight change by resisting it, or we can choose to become leaders, leading change and helping to shape the path for future generations.

Writing a book can seem so daunting, but I remembered why I began in the first place. As I remembered my 'why', my words began to flow with passion.

Your 'why' is the reason you get up every day with ambitions so strong.

Your why is who you're fighting for, why now matters more than ever, and why you simply can't back down.

Your why is for your parents, your friends, your kids, your grandkids, every person you see walking down the street, it's for the future of everything you love.

I'm fighting for the thousands of unemployed people around me, and the millions of small businesses failing every year globally.

I'm fighting for those who have helped me along the way, and those who are no longer here, let their lessons not be in vain. I'm fighting for our future generations, so they can avoid the struggles we've faced.

I'm fighting for those who have to work two or more jobs every day, those who realize they didn't save up enough money to be able to afford retirement, forced to continue working for the rest of their lives.

Most importantly, I'm fighting for you. An entrepreneur who believes in a better world and is willing to take the necessary steps to turn their vision into reality. May these lessons guide you on your path to success.

Remember, the odds you picked up this book and read it this far places you in 0.0001% of the world's population. You are unique. Don't let anyone tell you otherwise.

Stay in touch: Facebook.com/kkozakewich

Notes:

Notes:

NELSON CAMP

REAL ESTATE INVESTMENT AUTHORITY

Born in frigid Churchill, Canada, Nelson has since tried to warm the world with love, inspiration and encouragement. He has dedicated his life to enriching the lives of others through teaching, motivation, and encouragement. Along with his wife Kristine and their three children, they support many community organizations, volunteer their time, and generously give to many charities and good causes.

Nelson is an award-winning real estate investor, author, public speaker and high-level coach for those wanting to learn how to invest in real estate. He is the sole proprietor of a strong-producing portfolio of multi-family buildings, and the president and CEO of several companies, including the N-Gage Group of companies, Money Tree Academy, and Team Made Real Estate. Nelson is the winner of many awards, including Canadian Real Estate Wealth's Top Alternative Investor, and he was named one of the top 100 most influential people of North America by the John Maxwell Foundation and received the honor of Team Made Real Estate's People's Choice Award. He has been featured in *Canadian Real Estate Wealth Magazine* over a dozen times because of his expertise in real estate investing.

In addition to *FROM BROKE TO SUCCESS*, he is also an accomplished author of several books including: *Money Tree - How Anyone Can Become a Millionaire in 5 Years Through Real Estate* and *Thrive - A Collection of Short Pedagogical Plays*, and *Lifestyle by Design: A guide to Engineering the Life You've Always Wanted.*

He retired after a rewarding career of 20 years in formal education working as a teacher and guidance counselor. Nelson was awarded a master's degree in education and continues to bring value to others as a coach and a dynamic speaker in areas related to real estate, business, entrepreneurship, mental health, mindset, and motivation. He has a core goal of continuing to make a difference in the lives of others through empowerment, education and promoting lifestyle by design.

For more information on Nelson Camp or to book him for a speaking event, please visit www.nelsoncamp.com.

★★★★★

Now is the Time

Take a moment to stop what you're doing. Make sure you're outside and take a good look around. What do you see? If you're in an urban setting, you may see people, trees, cars, parks, and ... buildings — lots of buildings. If you look closer, you'll notice there are all kinds of buildings, big ones, small ones, those intended for people to live in, and those that have a retail or commercial purpose.

In all cases, the majority of the wealth around you is stored in buildings. Although many businesses are choosing to operate virtually, everyone still needs a place to live. There are only two choices for living accommodations, you either rent or you own. Your biggest monthly expense is likely the one related to housing and lodging – this is either a mortgage payment made to a financial institution or a lease payment made to your landlord.

Did you know that over 90% of the world's millionaires have used real estate as a major vehicle for creating wealth? If this many financially successful people have used real estate to establish wealth, why can't more? Why can't you? Since there is nothing around us that has greater monetary value than buildings and land, what's stopping you from owning more? In North America you can own as much real estate as you venture to buy. There is no limit imposed, so why not own more than your primary residence?

It's said that this industry is recession-proof, because even during a recession, everyone needs to live somewhere. That's what insulates this industry from a market downturn — the need to live somewhere will never disappear. The demand for housing will always exist, but the ratio between homeowners and renters does fluctuate. A wise investor knows that this is a key element to determining the cycle of the real estate market.

In North America, it's estimated by the rental-housing index that well over one third of the population rents rather than owns. Through both domestic growth and a constant stream of immigration coming to the US and Canada, the demand for rental properties will continue to rise. Providing good quality housing to those seeking to rent is a noble way of helping the community. As demographics continue to change across the continent, we are seeing more and more people choosing to rent rather than own to allow for a more nomadic lifestyle. Millennials are having fewer children, want to travel more, and to experience the freedom of being able to live anywhere in the world. This is an emerging market and movement that will continue to grow in popularity over the next decade, as the planet continues to become a smaller place, with the Internet, social media and the block chain.

We also see an aging population that is beginning to sell larger homes to downsize, and either look for condo living or rental living rather than owning. This allows the generation to access the wealth they accumulated in their primary residence and transfer this capital to living expenses for the later stages of their lives. Because of the transitions taking place, new opportunities in real estate will continue to manifest themselves.

Investing in real estate and becoming a millionaire is simple, but it isn't necessarily easy. In the following lessons, I will highlight some of the essential fundamentals to keep in mind if you want to grow a multi-million dollar portfolio of cash-producing assets.

★★★★★

Why You Need to Read This Section

Quite simply, you need to read this section in the book because I wrote it for you. Yes. For you!

When I started investing in real estate over ten years ago, I was alone. There were no books. There were no strategy guides. There were no online video tutorials. There were no real estate investment meet-up groups. The only thing that existed was the school of hard knocks. My admission to this unconventional institution of education was accepted and I spent a significant amount in tuition. This "school" believes in 100% field training and learning by doing. In other words, that means I had to learn the hard way through making mistakes. In real estate, we all know that you can make a great deal of income; but please don't forget you can also lose a lot of money. I have been very fortunate because I've made a lot of good choices and wise investments, but I have also learned many valuable lessons from unexpected events in real estate as well.

I wrote this book to teach you five lessons I have learned about real estate that have helped me become a multimillionaire. I want you to use some of the secrets that I discovered along the way, so that you too can be successful.

To be clear, I can't teach you to be a successful real estate investor in these five short lessons. But I can provide you with some vital theory to apply to your business model to increase your chances of success. If you want a user guide to help you develop a millionaire blue print, start with one of my other books: *Money Tree – How Anyone can Become a Millionaire in 5 Years Through Real Estate. Money Tree* is a great A-Z guide that will take you from developing mindset all the way to implementing a five-year millionaire plan.

If you're ready to take your game to the next level, read the following pages to discover some of the lessons I have learned about creating passive wealth through real estate investment, and how you too can apply them to your life.

★★★★★

Fill your Sails from Every Direction: Just Collecting Rent is for Beginners

Experienced sailors know that the wind is an important variable in determining both the speed of the ship, and the time it takes you to reach a destination. Based on the strength of the wind and the direction it is coming from, a sailor will adjust the sails accordingly. In most cases, several sails will be used to maximize the use of the winds. This allows for the ship to benefit from a variety of gusts and changes in wind in a collaborative fashion, to reach the destination faster. In the same way, real estate can be used several ways to create income and wealth.

Many people think investing in real estate is a pretty straightforward process: you buy a house and collect rent. At its core, this is the baseline of being a landlord. Anyone *can* buy a house and rent it, but not everyone becomes wealthy doing this. Not everyone knows how to capitalize on all the different streams of wealth created through the process of owning real estate. In this lesson, we will examine six different ways I have created wealth through owning real estate.

Anyone can buy a house and rent it, but not everyone becomes wealthy doing this

a) Rent Collection

Rent collection is what most people think of when they define what it means to be a landlord. Your rent is considered to be the income of your business, but keep in mind that the rent collected is simply the "gross income" of the landlord business model. There are also a variety of expenses that need to be taken into consideration when becoming a landlord to determine what your actual monthly profit is. This profit is called *cash flow*.

I have learned over the years the importance of proper planning of income and expenses on a building. Too often, investors will be seduced by the building or the deal, and skip through the financials. This is a huge pitfall and a necessary step that should not be overlooked when choosing a good investment for your money.

First and foremost, you will have your debt servicing, or your financing costs. In most cases, this will be the mortgage payment you make on the building, and will also be your biggest expense. That's why negotiating favorable terms with the lender is so important. In some cases, you may even have more than one mortgage registered on a property. However, that's not the only expense; there are also insurance costs, property taxes, perhaps HOA (homeowner association) fees, and there may be utility costs. Although these are the most common expenses associated with owning an investment property, there are others that are often forgotten or overlooked.

To start, it's important to include a monthly maintenance budget to allow for repairs, replacing a hot water tank, cutting the lawn or perhaps new shingles in several years. It's also prudent to plan a vacancy allowance. A vacancy allowance is accounting for the fact that there will eventually be a month with no tenant. Everyone will have a vacancy at some point. It's sometimes difficult to show or rent a suite that is occupied if the tenant's lifestyle prevents the space from showing well; it may be dirty, cluttered, unkept. A strategic and planned vacancy can allow for proper cleaning, improvements, to show the unit in its best condition, ultimately commanding the greatest possible rent. The final cost, that is often overlooked, is the cost of property management. It is possible that an investor will initially manage a rental property on their own, but it's important to include this cost as well for an eventual transition; time has value.

When you put together all of these numbers, you will be able to determine what the actual monthly profit is by subtracting all the expenses from the revenue.

The following table shows the financials from two different properties. Although the first property has less income than the second does, you can see that it is more profitable. As a matter of fact, the second property is not profitable at all; it actually loses money each month. This illustrates how important it is to properly examine and understand the yield of an investment.

	PROPERTY 1	**PROPERTY 2**
Income (Rent)	$1900	$2500
Taxes	$300	$425
Mortgage	$760	$1135
Insurance	$110	$145
Utilities	$60	$375
Vacancy	$95	$130
Management	$133	$182
Maintenance	$95	$130
Total Expenses	$1553	$2522
Profit	**$347**	**$-78**

b) Forced Appreciation

Forced appreciation is defined as the value added to a property through improving it. Many people have heard about "flipping houses" where a house is purchased for $100,000, they spend $30,000 in repairs and improvements, and then sell it for $200,000. The profit that is made between the incurred costs and selling price is the forced appreciation, but it's not necessary to be a flipper to benefit from the profit of improving a property.

It's possible to buy a distressed property, fix it up, and rent it for a much higher value than could have been achieved in its previous condition. This allows for more income but still benefits from the improved value. For example, you may buy a duplex for $200,000, improve it with $30,000 of work, and the new value of the property is $300,000. You have created $70,000 worth of value through forced appreciation. This amount is considered your wealth, and increases your net worth, but you don't immediately have access to this money as cash if you keep the building as an investment. If the building is sold, it can trigger capital gains taxes owed. If it isn't sold, the gain is non-taxable value left in the property until you sell it. However, it is possible to transfer this wealth into cash without triggering any taxes. We'll talk about this more in section e.

	PROPERTY 1 - Flip (Sold)	PROPERTY 2 - Refinance
Bought	$100,000	$100,000
Renovation	$20,000	$20,000
Total investment	$120,000	$120,000
Sold for	$160,000	
Refinance amount		$128,000 ($8,000 cash returned)
Yearly cashflow (post tax)		$3200
Taxes paid on sale	$10,000	
Cash flow after 5 years	$20,000	$16,000
Equity position after 5 years		$75,000
Gain after 5 years	**$20,000**	**$91,000**

c) Natural Appreciation

Over the last 150 years in North America, real estate has proven to be one of the wisest forms of investment. If you bought a house five years ago, the chances are very good that it's worth significantly more now. That difference in value is considered natural appreciation. The amount that a house will increase over the years is based on a number of factors including supply and demand, economy of the region, schools, access to transportation, and employers in the region among others. These are only a few of the numerous influencers of the rate of appreciation.

Some years, a region will see increases of over 10% or more (which would mean a $200,000 house grew in value by $20,000 within only one year!) or it may only see a gain of 1% (which would be only

$2,000 on the same $200,000 house). The commonality underlying natural appreciation is the general trend that real estate increases in value over the long-term. It's true there are years where a decline takes place, but for the most part, real estate increases in value.

Year	Value
Year 1	$210,000
Year 2	$220,500
Year 3	$231,525
Year 4	$243,101
Year 10	$325,779
Year 15	$415,786
Year 20	**$530,660**

* Based on a rate of appreciation of 5% per year

d) Mortgage Pay Down

Each month, an investor will have a mortgage payment. And this payment will come from the rent that is paid by the tenant. In a sense, the tenant is buying the investment property for the investor! In actuality, an investor doesn't pay off the property himself — the rental income does.

If a mortgage payment is $1000 per month, let's say $400 of that amount goes to the bank as interest on the mortgage, but the other $600 goes towards the principle owed on the house. Therefore, an investor is paying down the mortgage by $7200 each year ($600 x 12). Keep in mind that this amount continues to grow each year as less interest is paid and more principle is paid. This is wealth that is growing, adding to the investor's net worth each day passively – without doing anything at all other than owning the building and paying the mortgage with the revenue it generates. This amount is taxed as income, so when the property is sold, the equity created from the mortgage pay down will not trigger additional taxation.

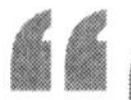

The investor will actually benefit from the growth of the entire value of the home and not just the portion invested.

e) Leverage

If an investment is made at the bank of $40,000 and they promise a 5% return, in one year, the profit generated is $2,000. However, how often does a bank guarantee a 5% return? It's not likely they will find a guaranteed investment at this rate because the growth rate of the capital is unknown. Even if you did, that amount is taxable as profit, so only a portion of it is kept. However, the rules of the game can change when real estate is purchased. With that same $40,000, a $200,000 duplex can be purchased ($40,000 would be the 20% down payment on this rental property). This investment may also grow by 5% in natural appreciation within one year. However, it won't only be the $40,000 that it grows. The investor will benefit from the growth of the entire value of $200,000 that grew by 5%: $10,000. That's five times more wealth created with the same $40,000 of seed money. The investor will actually benefit from the growth of the entire value of the home and not just the portion invested. This is the first benefit of using leverage. This sounds like an unfair advantage for real estate investors doesn't it? It certainly is — and the power of leverage can rocket launch net worth forward very quickly. This particular strategy is what made me a millionaire faster than anything else did. I was leveraging a small amount of seed money in each of my buildings to have growth based on the entire value of the portfolio of properties.

A savvy investor will know to find balance between leverage and equity.

There is a second benefit to the value of leverage. This means that the investor will have an equity position in a building that grows every year. Each month the property grows in value through natural appreciation, through forced appreciation and the mortgage is being paid down monthly. Eventually, you will be in a position where the home is worth much more than you owe. Therefore, if you owe $140,000 on a home that is worth $240,000, you can ask the bank to give you a portion of that equity of $100,000. This amount is not taxable until it is repaid to the bank and you can use it for a down payment to purchase another property. This is a second way you can use financial leverage to your advantage. The equity proceeds I have been able to withdraw from past purchases in the form of a line of credit (LOC) have been used as seed money for the down payment on other acquisitions. Eventually, a snowball effect happens when a critical mass is achieved, and all the buildings are growing in equity where they can be leveraged in rotation, if needed. It's important to remember to be wise in investment and not put yourself into a position where you are over-leveraged. A savvy investor will know to find balance between leverage and equity.

f) Tax advantages

Finally, there are many tax advantages to owning real estate for investment purposes. It's important to work closely with your accountant to determine the best tax-saving and tax-sheltering strategies you can use. This may include business expenses you incur to run your business, use of your vehicle, a home-based office, marketing expenses and renovation costs among other expenses.

So if you plan on driving a car, owning a house, buying a computer, along with other items you can declare as business expenses, why not benefit from the tax savings? One thing is certain; business owners and those who are self-employed get a definite advantage for tax planning and preparation regarding deductible business expenses.

It's also important to note that a property can be depreciated in value to allow the owner to shelter himself or herself from taxation. Keep in mind that the amount depreciated must later be recaptured when the property is sold, but it does allow for up-front tax savings until you choose to sell the property.

Value of $200,000	Appreciation	Mortgage paydown	Cash Flow
$20K renovation to increase value to $250K			
Year 1	$262,500	$155,625	$4,800
Year 2	$275,625	$151,117	$4,996
Year 3	$289,406	$146,473	$5,092
Year 4	$303,877	$141,688	$5,097
Year 10	$407,224	$109,788	$5,862
Year 15	$519,732	$78,487	$6,478
Year 20	$663,324	$42,160	$7,158
Total equity		$621,164	
Total Cash Flow			$119,334.87

* Based on a rate of appreciation of 5% per year

Once again, it's important to work with an experienced accountant who understands real estate investments, and can best advise you on tax planning.

These six pillars of wealth creation in real estate show why being a landlord is much more than just collecting rent. You can benefit from rent collection, forced appreciation, natural appreciation, mortgage pay down, leverage and a myriad of tax advantages.

With all of these forms of wealth generation put together, it's easy to see how it's possible to create over one hundred thousand dollars of wealth each and every year from just one property.

★★★★★

When Most Can't See the Forest Through the Trees: Find Opportunities Others Miss

Where do you live? Is it a continental region? Coastal? Near a forest? Close to the mountains? In the prairies? In an urban jungle? No matter where you live, you can become accustomed to the geographic uniqueness and actually no longer see opportunities because of familiarity. As someone who lives in the prairies, the beauty of mountains, the ocean, and forests profoundly affect me whenever I have an opportunity to travel. However, in the prairies, I see nothing but sky every day and rarely notice its beauty.

we can become accustomed to seeing opportunities all around us without actually noticing them

In the same way, we can become accustomed to seeing opportunities all around us without actually noticing them. Let's be honest with ourselves – like any other industry, the real estate market is competitive. There are many people looking for opportunities to succeed, and to create profit and wealth through strategic purchases. For the most part, flippers tend to look for the cheapest house or a damaged house. Investors tend to look for the finished rental properties that are producing good income. But this type of shopping is what most people do. If you want to find really good deals, you need to be more creative than what 90% of people are already doing.

The following chapter will outline some unique strategies that can be used to locate a more focused niche market that you can profit from, depending on what type of business model you follow.

a) Keywords

When searching online systems such as the MLS, Trulia, Craigslist, Kijiji or Zillow, many real estate flippers look for the least expensive houses. This can be an effective strategy when an entrepreneur is willing to accept a house that's rotten, has termites, foundation problems, no copper, or has simply reached the end of its life. It can be an opportunity to find teardown opportunities for those who enjoy building from scratch, but the challenge in this strategy is many people are already doing this.

In most real estate search engines, there is an option to search key words. It can be far more effective to find great opportunities by focusing on keywords rather than cheap properties. Here are a few great keywords to be searching to find hidden gems:

TLC – This seems pretty straightforward. A property needing TLC is often a building that requires work (Tender Loving Care), improvement, cleaning-up and finishing. Most homebuyers don't want to do the work and will pass this over. This provides a great opportunity for investors, contractors and flippers.

Estate – Using the keyword estate can allow you to find estate sales. This often happens when there has been a significant life transition for someone who has left a home. Sometimes it may be a death in the family or an illness. These sellers are often motivated and will want a quick sale. If you can close quickly with cash, you can often buy these buildings at a deep discount.

Motivated – A real estate agent will use the words motivated seller when they have a client who needs to sell fast. In most cases, even if a client is motivated, the agent doesn't want the public to know this because the buyer will think they can get a deal. When an agent takes the time to write "motivated" in the description, this often means that the seller is willing to cut losses and sell immediately. Motivated sellers will often take a price much lower than asking, to have the sale completed quickly. It's an indicator that the seller likely has a certain amount of desperation to sell.

Additional/Bonus – This can refer to an additional kitchen, a bonus suite, or extra attic space that can be developed into additional living space. These words often refer to something unique about the building that the right investor could capitalize on.

Price drop/Reduction – If a seller has dropped their price once, it is possible that they will be prepared to drop it a second time. This often shows that a seller is motivated to have their property purchased. If they dropped the price by $20,000 and you get it for an additional $20,000 less than the new asking price, you have made a purchase at $40,000 under the original asking price. This may allow you the profit you are looking for.

Handyman – The term handyman will come up when a building is in need of improvement. If someone is able to do some work on their own, they may be able to create a significant amount of forced appreciation into a building and also capitalize on a great price. Buildings that are damaged or unfinished can be difficult to finance traditionally, so a buyer with cash will be the only type of buyer that can purchase these buildings.

Special - This will often refer to a building that has some type of unique, or sought after quality, or feature. It can be a special price, a special layout, a special neighborhood or lot. There are a variety of unique characteristics that can be found when one searches for the word "special".

b) Out of place

When shopping for a good investment, it can be wise to search for a property that stands out from the rest in a particular neighborhood because of its price, its layout or its condition.

For example, if the bungalows or ranches in a certain area are selling for $300,000 and you find one particular house that's for sale at $185,000, you may have found a good potential investment. There may be hundreds of houses listed for under $150,000 in the same city, but in this particular neighborhood, this is the only property at a low price point. Keep in mind that this is regional and will change according to your location and the average pricing of homes.

It is also possible to find properties that stand out because of their layout. These can be properties that were converted or had additions built onto them. It's possible to find a property advertised as being 1,000 square feet, but when you look at the photos, you see an addition built that you're sure must not have been included in the square footage. This can be because permits were not granted or perhaps negligence on the real estate agent's behalf. In any case, the additional square footage may in fact increase the value of the property significantly and provide a good investment opportunity.

Finally, you can sometimes find a house that stands out because of its condition. Have you heard the old saying "Buy the worst house on the best street"? This is sometimes true for finding a good opportunity. A house may stand out from all the rest because it hasn't been maintained or properly updated throughout the years, compared to all the neighboring properties. Some quick cosmetic work can often create an opportunity for profit.

I once went to see an abnormally large house in an area where other houses were smaller in square footage. It turned out that the house was actually a multi-family dwelling that was being incorrectly marketed by the real estate agent. Upon doing some due-diligence, I discovered that the property was in fact a 3-unit building and not a single family dwelling, as most people had believed. This unique perspective allowed me to purchase a home-run deal that many other investors had passed-over. Restoring it to three units allowed for an increase in value of over $150,000!

c) Conversions

One strategy that is overlooked by the majority of investors is the ability to convert an existing home's use to increase its value. Similar to the example used in b) above, a wise real estate investor will be able to identify single-family homes that may have the potential to be used as a multi-unit properties. Doing this will have a positive impact on the home as a rental; rather than renting a 3 bedroom 2 bathroom for $1500/mo., it may be possible to rent a 2-1 for $1,000/mo. and a 1-1 for $850/mo. This can increase the rent generated by $350 per month or $4,200 per year. In addition to this, it can increase the value of the property. In some markets, duplexes will be valued for more than similar-sized single-family homes. Thus, you may be able to create a significant amount of value to a home by changing its use.

When considering the possibility of converting a building to more than one suite, there are a few key elements to look for. The first is the general layout of the building. For example, is there a natural split between the upper and main levels? Is there a natural split between the main floor and basement? Where are the staircases located? Is there easy to access plumbing for both a kitchen and a bathroom?

A second important factor to consider is separate entrances since each unit will require its own designated entrance. Does the building have a front door and back door? Is there a side door? How close are stairs to the entrances?

When converting a home, it's important to adhere to all zoning regulations and ensure proper work permits are granted for the work that is to be done. If you're not sure about the proper steps to follow when converting a building, it's always a good idea to check with your municipality to confirm the requirements.

This particular method has helped me to create hundreds of thousands of dollars of equity through property conversions and it should not be over-looked as a sophisticated method of creating value in the real estate market.

d) Higher end homes

Another area that is often over looked by flippers is the higher end market. Although the norm is to sell houses in the most sought-after price range of a particular region, some select flippers will seek out higher end homes and will bank on a larger return rather than volume.

In many markets, there is an opportunity to buy the worst house in higher-end neighborhoods and bank on the location. For example, if you purchase a house for $720,000 in a neighborhood where houses all sell for a million dollars or more, it may be possible to renovate for $130,000 in improvements and still make a sizeable profit.

> *to be successful, it's important to have a business model that stands out.*

Caution should be exercised when entering this market because the price point for purchasing entails potentially having quite costly carrying costs associated with high taxes, insurance costs, and especially debt servicing.

The common thread in all of these unique strategies is to do something different from everyone else. Like any market, investing in real estate can be quite competitive; to be successful, it's important to have a business model that stands out.

e) Zoning issues

A final area that is often overlooked is the particular niche of houses in a neighborhood where zoning issues may provide some unique opportunities. Particular neighborhoods will have land designation that allows homes to be used as duplexes (or two-family dwellings), or triplexes (three-family dwellings), or even for commercial purposes.

A sophisticated investor will see an opportunity to buy a building that is currently being used as a single-family dwelling but had previously been declared as a multi-family building. Knowing this seems to be an unfair advantage once again, because the sophisticated investor can do his or her homework in determining if the building can easily be returned to its original state of accommodating more than one living unit.

In the right market, this can quickly and easily allow for a building to experience forced appreciation through simply changing its use. For example, a single-family dwelling may be selling for

$200,000 for a 1000 sq. ft. home. However, if commercial buildings of similar square footage are selling for $270,000, it may be an opportunity to modify the buildings use with minimal investment.

In summary, this would be considered doing a flip by changing the building use. Although this may seem like a small change, it can have a big impact. The following lesson will address other ways of making small changes for big results.

Small Changes = Big Results: The 10% Tweak

In the following lesson I outline some creative strategies to use when analyzing a potential acquisition, or to improve an existing portfolio. Being able to objectively look at a business model and determine where costs can be cut and revenue can be increased is not only a science, but also an art. Sometimes, a little fine-tuning is all that's required to turn a bad investment into a good investment. This lesson will highlight some creative methods of tweaking a building that I have used to make it a winner.

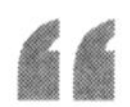

Sometimes, a little fine-tuning is all that's required to turn a bad investment into a good investment

a) Increase income by 10% - increase rent, or add services or amenities that add value, like offering storage, a garden, or additional parking.

It doesn't sound like much, but an increase of 10% in the income generated by a business is sometimes the tipping point for changing everything. The effect of the change will be compounded over months, years and eventually will have a much more profound impact.

Let's say we have a four unit building that is composed of two two-bedroom units and two one-bedroom units. Currently, the rent is $1000/mo. for the two-bedroom suites and $850/mo. for the one-bedroom suites. This represents a monthly income of $3700 or $44,400 a year. Finding a way to increase the income by 10% can have an important impact on the bottom line. This can be done several different ways. The most obvious method of increasing the income is to increase the rent values. If the current rents are below market value, you may be able to increase the rent you fetch for the existing suites. It's important to follow all legislation in your region, state, province or territory to ensure that rent changes are done in a proper fashion.

There are other ways to increase the income as well, if your current rents are already fair for the market in which you find yourself. Here are some creative strategies that can be used to increase the income:

Laundry – Offering laundry services to tenants is a great way to allow for additional revenue. Although coin-operated laundry can be an investment up front, it is a tax-deductible expense and will allow for more income to be generated. Consequently, it can also reduce expenses on water and energy - when a tenant is required to pay for their laundry, they become more responsible for the amount of loads they do.

Storage – Never underestimate the value in storage. People will always have seasonal items that they need to put somewhere and the back of a bedroom closet is rarely the answer! The list of items that need proper storage is endless: the Christmas tree, a bike, a boogie board, seasonal clothing, skis, etc. Is there space to build lockers? Storage lockers off site will be expensive and a pain for the tenant. If you can offer a more affordable and convenient option to your clients, they may jump at the chance to rent this additional service.

Parking – Not everyone has a vehicle, but those that do have one recognize that there can be several costs associated. Gas, insurance, maintenance and parking are all part of the responsibility of having a vehicle. If you have indoor or outdoor parking available, you can offer it first to tenants and then after to community members. Even if your tenants aren't interested in the parking, someone else from the neighborhood may have a seasonal vehicle, boat, RV, or want a garage for mechanical work. Be creative about how your parking generates income.

Convert a unit – Some units can be converted to maximize their profitability. For example, you may have a suite that has an eat-in kitchen and formal dining area. If you don't feel you are able to fetch additional rent by offering the dining area, you could create an additional bedroom in that space and then charge a higher rent for this suite. Your spacious one bedroom suite just became a cash-producing 2-bedroom unit!

Garden – More and more, society is recognizing the importance of organic food and produce grown at home. In many urban areas, citizens will pay monthly fees to use a small parcel of land in community gardens. These gardens rarely have access to water and someone may have to drive to the outskirts of the city to tend to them. If you are able to offer a garden to tenants or neighbors in the middle of an urban environment, you may find yourself with a new form of revenue!

b) Increase volume by 10%

A volume increase would be beneficial for those growing a portfolio. Depending on your business model, your main focus may not be cash flow. Some investors prefer to invest in mass volume to benefit from a larger amount of natural appreciation and mortgage pay down simultaneously. For example, if you have 10 rental units you could simply add one more property or even a duplex to boost up the volume by 10% or 20% with the extra doors.

However, don't forget that this volume increase will also have an impact on your natural appreciation, your mortgage pay down and your income.

If your current portfolio consists of 10 doors and is valued at 1 million, a natural appreciation of 10% would yield a growth of $100,000 a year. This amount can very quickly increase by acquiring an additional building valued at $200,000. This would increase your natural appreciation by $20,000 a year. In turn, your mortgage pay down amount will likely increase by $6000 a year or more. When you put all this together, you can see why increasing volume by just one building can yield significant gains.

c) Decrease expenses by 10%

Not only is it important to increase income, but it's also important to be able to effectively decrease the expenses incurred in the operation of a real estate business. This is called the art of leaning. The biggest risk for real estate investors is vacancy. If a suite goes empty for only one month, that amount can represent an important percentage of income that was not earned for a given year.

Although it's not possible to completely avoid vacancies, it is possible to be proactive in preventing them. Ensuring effective management and maintaining a good, open dialogue with tenants can tip you to upcoming vacancies. Also, working with a skilled property manager can be helpful; they very often have several potential tenants that they are working with and seeking housing for. This can be especially useful when an unexpected vacancy comes up. If your property manager has several pre-screened tenants waiting for the right place, he or she may be able to avoid a vacancy all together.

But this art of leaning or reducing expenses, doesn't only apply to vacancies. There are many other ways to trim your costs. Here are a few ways of bringing down the cash being spent to allow more revenue to be kept.

Separate utilities – If you have a multi-unit building, it may be wise to invest some capital up front to allow for long-term savings. By adding electrical meters for each suite, you are allowing your tenants to take responsibility for their own consumption. This can be particularly wise in regions where units have their own form of heating and cooling, because climate management tends to be one of the most expensive costs that landlords incur. All new acquisitions in my portfolio go through an evaluation to determine what utility costs can be passed onto the tenant. When a tenant is responsible for their utility use, they tend to be wiser in consumption and therefore become better stewards of the environment.

Reduce taxes – Property taxes often represent a significant expense for the building owners. In many regions, it is possible to appeal the cost of taxes and have them reduced, if there are grounds to do this. To dispute property taxes it will be important to ensure proper due diligence ahead of time, to justify to the municipal government why you feel that you are being over-charged, based on comparable properties in the neighborhood.

Insurance policy – Property insurance is the cost that nobody wants to pay for when things are going well but is the most important expense if a claim must be made. It is important to regularly review the policy you have in place and determine if it's the most cost-effective way of protecting your investments. You may be surprised to see what types of alternative insurance coverage exists. It's free to ask competitors to offer you a quote. Ensure you are comparing apples to apples when examining policies and liability inclusions.

Low maintenance – Grounds keeping can be an ongoing monthly expense that never goes away. Have you done a "low-maintenance" audit on your properties to see if there's a way to reduce costs associated with cutting the lawn, watering plants, and pulling weeds? Perhaps there is a way to modify the landscaping so that weekly maintenance isn't required and only monthly maintenance is needed? This can include drought resistant plants, hardscapes rather than lawn, and perhaps dwarf bushes that grow to a maximum size and don't require trimming.

Systems - Effective systems are a sure way of being able to lean costs. Redundancies in any type of business model are often significant drains on resources and capital.

For example, if you have a portfolio that is spread in different regions of a city, it may be wise to arrange for preventative maintenance in one region at a time, rather than driving in between several in one day and paying a crew for hours of driving. Or perhaps you have a painting crew that does all the painting at once, rather than invite them several times a year where you get a call-out fee. It's wise to consider automating processes such as rent collection or maintenance requests. It will also save an enormous amount of time and headaches by having a master key system, a well-put together tenant manual, and systems for move-ins, move-outs, marketing, etc. Finally, it's beneficial to be continuously working on your business plan to streamline operations, improve efficiencies and ultimately reduce your costs in terms of financial resources as well as time.

d) Pay off mortgages 10% faster – extra income can pay mortgages down much faster

Did you know that you could pay off your mortgage faster? Depending on the terms of your debt servicing arrangements, you may be able to increase your mortgage payments and also put lump sums towards the mortgage. If your ultimate goal is not cash flow, you may want to consider paying down mortgages faster than the original amortization period of 20, 25 or 30 years. In the long run, you will save money in interest expenses but will have less cash flow. You decide what your business models calls for.

In some cases, you may want to sell one property that has significant growth in equity to pay down (or pay off) other mortgages. Or perhaps the capital created will be used for seed money in additional acquisitions. It's important to determine the best strategies to use to ensure you are also taking your tax exposure into consideration when buying/selling and paying down mortgages. The interest portion of a mortgage payment is tax deductible and represents a large business expense. No longer having a mortgage can mean more income, but more taxes to pay as well; always work closely with your accountant to determine what strategy will best meet your needs for short term and long-term growth.

When looking at options to tweak your portfolio, 10% is often all it takes to see a big difference. Whether it's 10% more clients, 10% more revenue, or 10% less in expenses — all these methods will improve your bottom line. What's most interesting is when you apply all of these levers at once, to see what the ultimate outcome is for your business. Watch how the profit windfall starts with just a few minor adjustments.

	10% income	**10% more clients**	**10% less expenses**
Starting Value	$150,000	15 units	$90,000
10%	$15,000	1.5 (round to 2)	$9,000
Total	**$165,000**	**17 units**	**+$9,000 cash flow**

★★★★★

Plant Your Seeds Wisely: If You Don't Sow You Won't Have Anything to Reap

After a long winter season, spring is always a welcome change. It's a time when trees come back to life, birds lay their eggs, and gardens are planted. When planting, the gardener knows that each seed is representative of the plant that will grow, and ultimately the fruit or vegetables it will bear.

The gardener also knows that each seed is representative of the miracle of multiplication. One simple seed can produce a plant with many fruits and vegetables. For this reason, no farmer will plant only one seed and care for it exclusively. A wise farmer will plant many seeds and care for all of them through implemented systems, to ensure they are all producing and nurtured.

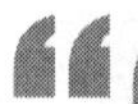

The single greatest decision I made when growing my portfolio was to stretch myself as far as possible at the beginning

When investing in real estate, there are a few important factors to keep in mind when planning your strategy and using your seed money. The reality is that you will always eventually run out of your own capital, so planning ahead ensures you will be able to move your real estate investing business forward.

The single greatest decision I made when growing my portfolio was to stretch myself as far as possible at the beginning, to purchase as many properties as I was able to. Although this meant living frugally initially, to spend generously in my business, the law of multiplication was quick to produce incredible returns in many properties rather than just one.

a) Spread the seed out

When planting a garden, it's best to spread the seed out in a way that allows multiple plants to grow simultaneously. Similarly, it is wise to spread capital over many properties at the same time rather than invest it all into one venture.

For example, if you only have $100,000 to invest in real estate, it may be prudent to spread this amount into more than one property to maximize the growth potential of your portfolio. There are several creative ways to do this.

Down payment – By moving into the building for a period of time, the banks will often require a much smaller down payment (5%). This is much better than when a property is strictly purchased as an investment because, in this case, the bank will most often require 20%-25% as a down payment. On a $200,000 house, the difference is significant: $10,000 would be a 5% down payment and $50,000 would be a 25% down payment. This strategy is sometimes referred to as a house-hack.

This method of moving into a house first can be repeated multiple times to allow for a more efficient spread of initial capital. It's important to check with local tax laws regarding how long you are required to occupy the property for it to be considered your primary residence.

Equity position – In some cases, you may be able to have an equity position in a building from the get-go. For example, if you purchase a building for $200,000 that is in fact worth $250,000 as a fair market value, it may be in your interest to first purchase the building in cash with private money and then seek financing from a bank at the appraised value of $250,000. In most cases, a bank will lend you 80% of the appraised value or $200,000 towards the property. This would be considered a no-money down acquisition, as the initial investment of $200,000 would be issued as a first mortgage on the property that you purchased for this same amount!

Vendor take back – In some cases, a seller may consider offering a second mortgage on the property at a higher interest rate. For example, he or she may agree to lend the equivalent of the down payment (20%). This would be considered a deal where there are two mortgages on a building - the first mortgage would be from the bank at 80% of the value, and the second would be from the seller at 20% of the value. This would once again be a "no-money down" deal.

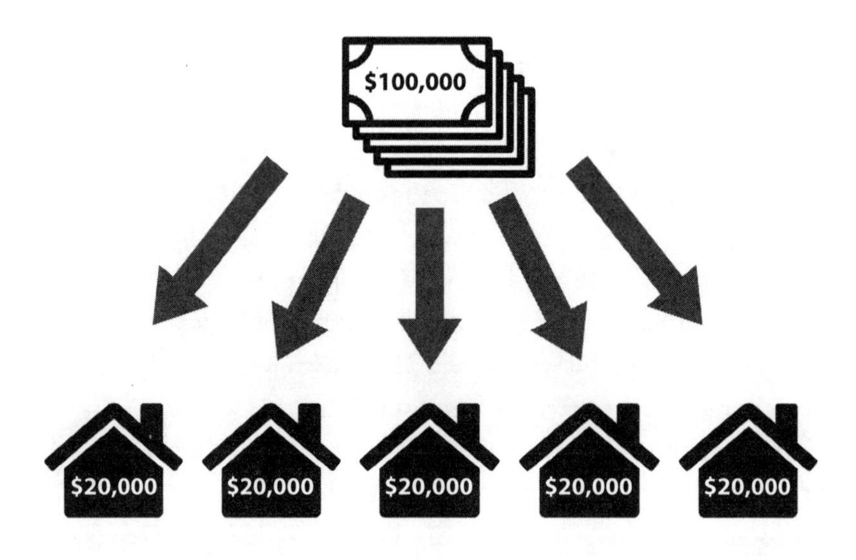

b) Tend to your seed

Once you have a seed planted, the next step is to ensure it is cared for. It must be watered, exposed to sunlight, pruned, and fertilized.

Similar to an investment property, the owner will need to tend to maintenance, pay the bills, and manage the building and tenants with excellence to ensure the building continues to produce revenue while staying in good condition. Many absent landlords have been surprised that the condition of their buildings and the quality of the clients can quickly deteriorate when they are not directly involved with the management.

c) Know when to harvest

Each type of plant has an optimal maturity date or time when the fruit or vegetables are ready to be picked. If it's picked too early, it may not be ready to eat. If it's picked too late, it may start to rot or no longer be good to eat.

When buying a property, it's important to consider what the goal of the property is and when it will be sold. This is called the exit strategy and should be an important element in the planning of a building.

Here are a few examples of times and exit strategies:

Short term – A short-term hold may be up to one year. This would include houses that are purchased, improved, and sold immediately, or may also be related to a house purchased in a neighborhood that is seeing very fast appreciation. If the investor's goal is to have liquid cash, this may be a wise exit strategy. Keep in mind, when a property is sold, it triggers tax to pay on the revenue generated or the capital gains.

Midterm - A midterm hold would be considered anything up to five or even 10 years. This will often coincide with the mortgage renewal. Rather than renewing the mortgage, the investor may decide to sell the property and keep the cash flow it has generated for five years or ten years along with any equity that has grown in the property.

Long term – A long-term hold is considered to be up to the maturity date of the mortgage. When the mortgage is completely paid off, the property begins to produce a significant amount of profit because the biggest expense (debt servicing) has been eliminated. Depending on income planning, the investor may at this point choose to refinance the property into a new mortgage to access the equity of the building without paying taxes on the capital that the loan yields. Alternatively, the investor may choose to sell the property and pay the tax due. Estate planning with an accountant should be an important factor that is considered before selling.

Indefinite – An indefinite hold is a property where there is no intention of selling. The most common way of holding this property will be in corporation. The reason being is that a corporation can have different shareholders who benefit from income or dividends and the business is technically immortal – it will never die. If a property is held personally by an individual or partners, they will eventually die and the estate will be responsible for paying tax regardless of whether the building is disposed of or not. In some cases, individuals will transfer personal holdings into a holding corporation as they age, to trigger the tax before they die and then allow the corporation to hold the property and pay out other shareholders perpetually. It's important to discuss proper estate planning and financial planning with a knowledgeable accountant and lawyer. You'll find your time and money are well invested when working with the right professionals on your team.

Writing Offers Like No One Else Does: Pro-Conditions to Use When Writing an Offer to Purchase

One thing is certain in real estate: if you write no offers, you will always miss 100% of the opportunities that present themselves. It's an undeniable truth.

When you ask a struggling investor, who is having no luck in finding a good deal, how many offers they wrote last week, they will most often tell you "none". No one wants to live with regrets. Taking action allows you to conquer fear. Fear can get you locked up in indecision and can also cause you to make the wrong decisions.

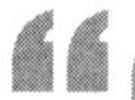

Taking action allows you to conquer fear.

The best deals are created and orchestrated – they don't magically appear. It is through negotiation, relationships, and follow-up that professional level investors manage to get "homerun deals" under contract. It is possible for a great deal to be brought to you from a lead, but very often, you will need to hunt for your next acquisition. When you find the right seller who is motivated to sell a property, it's an opportunity to structure a creative win-win deal and produce some profit for yourself. This can be in the form of equity, cash flow or capital, depending on your financial goals. This takes time, effort, and commitment. It also takes consistent, actionable steps. All these ingredients put together will position an investor to orchestrate many successful deals.

But most people don't know how to be creative in writing offers. Even realtors, who are supposed to be experts in writing offers, don't always have the knowledge and experience to write offers using a creative method that encourages a seller to accept an offer. The next lesson will outline some strategies to use when writing offers to get a greater number accepted and to find value in unique ways. There will also be some wise negotiation tactics to use when closing a deal.

a) Price – When you want to buy a house, there are several different numbers that rise to the surface. The first is the *list price* or the *asking price*; that's the price a seller is advertising as desired for their property. It's like the regular price on an item at a store, except in real estate there is no rule that says you need to pay that price. You are welcome to make an offer for whatever you want and the seller will respond. It is possible to get a deep discount on a property by simply offering a lower price than asking. This is especially useful when a property has been listed on the market for an extended period of time, or perhaps the vendor is anxious or very motivated to sell.

In some cases, a vendor will be getting transferred to another city and will have an agreement from their employer that if the house sells for less than listed price, the employer will pay the owner the difference. This happens very often with big corporations and military personnel. In that situation, you can take advantage of a quick sale at a deep discount. The final price agreed to is the *sale price.*

In between the two, there's something called the accepted price. That's not the initial price. You can have an offer accepted subject to inspection, and after you have a property inspection, you are permitted to renegotiate the price.

For example, let's imagine a building is listed for $200,000 and you write an offer for $175,000 with the condition of a satisfactory property inspection. After the inspection, you go back to the seller, mention your laundry list of items, tell them you can only do the deal if they split the $30,000 cost of work you estimated, and you are willing to pay $160,000 only. They may accept that or counter with a different number. In almost all cases, they will come down again if you justify the further discount. And perhaps the price you pay will be $160,000 or $165,000. In both cases, you receive a significant discount from the asking price.

b) Possession date - Buyers often don't realize how much value there can be in a possession date. This can vary depending on the market you are investing in. There are a variety of ways to use a possession date to your advantage, in both flip projects and in buy and hold acquisitions; let's examine a few.

Natural Appreciation – In markets where there is strong appreciation, you can create a significant profit for yourself by giving a buyer their price, but setting your own possession date.

Let's imagine a buyer is looking for $300,000 in a market that's appreciating at 15% per year. That means that this building is appreciating at $45,000 per year, or almost $4,000 per month. If you can push a possession date back by 4 months, you can potentially create a profit of $16,000 of natural appreciation on the deal.

Most investors don't realize that this alone can result in a *buy, stage and sell.* With very little improvement done to the building it can be sold for a small profit, without a large engagement of work committed to the acquisition.

It should be noted that this strategy can in fact be dangerous should the market fundamentals change. A market will not stay in a constant state of rapid appreciation indefinitely. Caution must be used when banking solely on appreciation.

Close quickly - In some cases, a seller may have already left their home and they are living in their new home. That means that they are quite possibly paying for two mortgages, two sets of property taxes, two insurance policies (including one being an expensive vacant building policy) and two sets of utilities. This can be extremely stressful for a seller and they may be motivated to take a lesser price, with the knowledge that the house will be sold quickly. This type of peace of mind will sometimes translate into saving tens of thousands of dollars on the buy price. The down side is they will have to wait up to 6 weeks for the funds from the new mortgage to come through. This brings us to the option to close quickly with cash and application of a second "pressure-point."

Close quickly with cash – The only thing better than closing quickly with a motivated seller is closing quickly with cash. When a seller needs to sell quickly and they are supporting two different homes, they will want money fast. You can get a discount to close quickly and even further negotiate to get an additional discount to close the deal with cash in 10 days — typically, a seller can wait four, or even six weeks for the funds from a mortgage to be advanced.

Avoiding certain bills – It's strategically wise to consider this when you are buying a home. Statistically, the best times of year to make offers on a house (worst times to sell) are in November and December. Most people are focused on Christmas and holidays and have very little interest in buying, and even less interest in moving during the colder months. That means there are opportunities for buyers who are looking for a good deal.

It's also a great way to postpone a possession until the spring, when heating bills will be minimal or non-existent. This translates to the seller being responsible for any bills associated with heating, and the property remains the risk of the current owner until possession date arrives. It can be quite costly to replace a boiler or furnace and if they fail prior to possession, the onus will be upon the vendor to repair or replace them, to ensure the mechanical systems are in good working order if the offer to purchase stipulates this. This will save you money on utilities, while you still benefit from the value of the property increasing through natural appreciation.

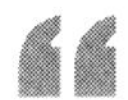

The human brain is an amazing tool but it has some default settings that allow it to operate without much user input.

c) Offer A or B

As a general rule, people never stop to think about the way human psychology works. The human brain is an amazing tool but it has some default settings that allow it to operate without much user input. Being able to better understand human psychology and the psychology of decision-making will give you an unfair advantage in writing offers, and in negotiation.

When you ask someone a yes/no question, the expected answer is also yes or no. However, there is no rule that says you can't ask an "A or B" question, also known as an "or" question, when buying a house. More specifically, you can make someone more than one offer for their home at the same time. One may have a higher deposit than the second. One may have a further possession date than the second. One may have a higher price than the second. As soon as you give someone two choices, they forget that "no" is still a viable answer.

Their brain automatically defaults to choosing one over the other and tries to best determine which one they like the most. The job of the buyer is to ensure that both offers written are acceptable to him or her, and that they can create value in both of them.

d) Wolf Pack Strategies – Make Something Ugly Attractive; You and I BOTH Offer

Have you ever observed the way a pack of wolves attacks its prey? It happens in a very calculated fashion; several wolves will converge silently from different directions upon their prey. One wolf will first show himself to scare the prey in the opposite direction, where there will be several other wolves waiting to make the kill. Even though the first wolf is not responsible for the kill, his role is no less important, and he will get to share in the meal.

In a similar fashion, you can work in cooperation with other investors to get your offer accepted. This strategy can be useful when you think a seller will reject your offer without even counter-offering. The strategy is as follows: you want to make your ugly low-ball offer appear "not so bad". To do this, you will work with another investor and both inform the listing agent or seller that you are bringing an offer. In no way do you let the seller know that you are both known to one another. Your offer is low, but your colleague's offer is *very* low. The seller gets to see both offers at the same time, or preferably your colleague's *very* low offer slightly before your low offer. The seller will see the other offer first and laugh or be offended, but then he or she sees yours and realizes that it's much more reasonable than the first.

Once again, the seller will be faced with two offers to choose from, and of course, yours will be the only reasonable option, even though if it would have been presented alone it would have been deemed unreasonable. Having a terrible offer presented at the same time as a very low offer increases the chances of the low offer being accepted.

e) As-is

A wise investor knows that many people view cash as king. Human nature tends to default to people being lazy, greedy, and fearful, in most cases. That means that if someone is faced with an opportunity to do something the easy way or the hard way, they will likely do it the easy way. When writing an offer, you can determine to what level the vendor is "lazy" by conditions (or lack of conditions) in an offer. In some cases, a vendor will be shocked to see an offer with no conditions and a tight deadline for acceptance. This would be an offer accepting the home "as-is" and if the vendor signs the offer, the deal must proceed to closing. If a vendor is motivated by "laziness", they may accept the offer to avoid having to go and find another buyer, and be confident that the deal is firm.

In the same way, the human characteristic called greed is an important lever to use when making an offer. Greed can be viewed in two different fashions: one perception is that greed means someone wants the most, more than others, and to keep it to themselves. It is also said that greed is closely related to impatience. That means that a vendor may want their money *right away* and not want to wait. Being aware of this allows a buyer to present an "as-is" cash offer where the vendor will not need to wait to have financing approved, inspections approved, a delayed negotiation process or the fear of having to find another buyer. Proceeds from a mortgage can sometimes take weeks to be transferred. If a seller wants their money right away, they may be more inclined to accept a lower price, but know they are selling their property for cash, and that they will have their money within two or three days rather than potentially several weeks.

The reader is cautioned about writing offers "as-is". If a vendor accepts your offer as written, it will not allow for a contingency plan if anything new is discovered down the road. The vendor will also be entitled to legally keep the entire deposit that is submitted with the offer to purchase. If for some reason the buyer is not able to purchase the home on the closing date, the vendor may be able to sue the buyer as well, for non-performance as outlined in the contract. It is strongly recommended to have a detailed conversation with your lawyer and an experienced real estate investor prior to engaging in writing "as-is" offers.

★★★★★

For Every Entrepreneur

No matter where you are on this journey, we hope you are feeling motivated to take charge of tomorrow and take action! Are you ready to start your journey to success and step into a world of financial freedom?

The only obstacle that prevents you from achieving your full potential is your mindset. Don't let fear, doubt, or excuses be the author of your future. Take charge of your destiny and decide to make the rest of your life be the best of your life!

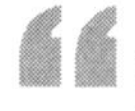

> *Take charge of your destiny and decide to make the rest of your life be the best of your life!*

If you want to learn more about real estate investing and creative ways to grow your business, you may want to read my book entitled *Money Tree: How Anyone Can Become a Millionaire in 5 Years Through Real Estate*. It's an A-Z guide that will help you learn the moving parts involved in becoming a successful investor. This book is written for anyone interested in learning how to become an investor, or for those who are learning and want to focus on improving their business model. It also unpacks actionable steps and timelines to help you plan to become a millionaire in five years. Yes. It is possible to become a millionaire in five years or less.

Perhaps you're looking for education? Don't want to take the time to produce all your own documents, materials and systems? I invite you to visit **www.moneytree.academy** to find a variety of resources, articles, documents, videos, user-guides, and other tools to make you a successful real estate investor. Watch videos that will guide you step-by-step along the path of learning to create wealth through real estate. Rather than developing your own materials, download proven templates of hundreds of documents that you can add to your business systems.

Would you like to improve the lifestyle you find yourself living? You may want to read my book entitled *Lifestyle by Design: A Guide to Engineering the Life You Want.* This book will help you examine all the different areas of your life and determine where you need improvement. Have you ever thought about being "work optional"? That's the amazing checkpoint you reach when you no longer have to work because you are financially independent, but you can choose to work if you find it fulfilling. Or perhaps you want more rewarding relationships? Better health? Whether it's benefiting from a passive income lifestyle or living in optimal health, this book will guide you toward changing your entire mindset and then taking action.

Finally, if you would like to connect further, you can do so by following me on social media. You can also visit www.nelsoncamp.com to contact me or to access personalized mentorship and coaching.

Notes:

Notes:

Notes: